Conversations
with
Manuel Castells

Manuel Castells and Martin Ince

polity

First published in 2003 by Polity Press in association with Blackwell Publishing Ltd

Editorial office:
Polity Press
65 Bridge Street
Cambridge CB2 1UR, UK

Marketing and production:
Blackwell Publishing Ltd
108 Cowley Road
Oxford OX4 1JF, UK

Distributed in the USA by
Blackwell Publishing Inc.
350 Main Street
Malden, MA 02148, USA

Library of Congress Cataloging-in-Publication Data
Castells, Manuel.
Conversations with Manuel Castells / Manuel Castells and Martin Ince.
p. cm.
Includes bibliographical references and index.
ISBN 0-7456-2848-6 – ISBN 0-7456-2849-4 (pbk.)
1. Castells, Manuel. 2. Sociologists – Interviews. I. Ince, Martin, 1952- II. Title.
HM479.C37 C65 2003
2002153726

Typeset in 11 on 13 pt Berling
by SNP Best-set Typesetter Ltd., Hong Kong
Printed and bound in Great Britain by TJ International, Padstow, Cornwall
For further information on Polity, visit our website: www.polity.co.uk

Contents

Acknowledgments

I would like to thank John Thompson and Gill Motley of Polity for their support of this book, which they conceived and commissioned as part of a series of conversations with leading social scientists. But principally I would like to thank Manuel Castells himself for his hard work on this project and for his friendship, which has survived the sometimes difficult process of creating this book. It was Manuel's decision to suggest me as an author who would engage intellectually with the complex subject matter of his work from a perspective outside the social sciences. He has made it clear throughout the project that he regards himself as the "object" and me as author, responsible for the structure of the book as well as the detailed questions in each conversation. I had previously interviewed him at length by email, giving us both confidence that this *modus operandi* would work and be enjoyable, and I have very much enjoyed the opportunity for serious intellectual exchange that this project has provided. In addition, I would like to thank Manuel, and Emma Kiselyova, for their hospitality in Barcelona.

Martin Ince

Manuel Castells in Siena, in 1994, at the time of the writing of *The Rise of the Network Society*. Photograph by Emma Kiselyova.

Introduction

Manuel Castells is one of the world's best-known social scientists. His renown extends far beyond the academic arena which is his lifelong home. Politicians, business executives, labor leaders, NGO activists, journalists and opinion-formers of all kinds are among those interested in his work, while his standing in many scholarly communities is authoritative, and he ranks high in the Social Science Citation Index. In October 2000 the *Observer* newspaper listed him as the 139th most influential person in Britain, ahead of Baroness Thatcher and an array of contemporary leaders of business, politics, and the media – impressive indeed for someone who lives in California and Catalonia.

As the bibliography of this book shows, Manuel's work has ranged far from his doctoral dissertation on industrial location, in which he studied high-technology firms in the Paris region, although an interest in the geography of economic development has been one constant of his career.

His interests have become as broad as his travels, which began, as he tells us in conversation 1, with his first political exile, from his homeland of Spain.

His wide-ranging interests mean that there are many reasons to want to know about him and his work. He is one of the few academics with a substantial following among people working in business, because of his detailed analysis of new information technology. His work has also informed the thinking of trade union leaders, as his May 1st Award for

Social Thought, received from the Catalan trade unions in 1999, shows. In the same year he received an award for his work on the Internet from the Catalan Chambers of Commerce and Industry, a double achievement whose rarity acknowledges the special status of his work.

The sweep of his insights into how societies work and how they change means that his work is also of interest to politicians – for the most part not immense readers – who perhaps recognize in him someone who could be a considerable politician in his own right but has taken a life decision not to compete with them. His early life, as an anarchist and a left-winger, is now behind him. He is still a committed citizen in terms of his values, and places himself on the independent Left, but he refuses to let his research and analysis be biased by politics. He says, "Truth in itself is revolutionary, because it empowers people at large with an understanding of their lives and their world."

His emphasis on the importance of less formal politics also broadens the interest of, and in, his work. He has stressed the significance of nongovernmental organizations and of citizen organization, a theme of his massive study *The City and the Grassroots* (1983), and has extended his work into the era of globe-encompassing NGOs in fields such as the environment, development, and human rights. His analysis has some unexpected followers. A Muslim military leader in Chechnya, interviewed by Netherlands television about his motivation, waved a heavily annotated copy of *The Information Age* and declared: "This is what we are fighting against!" The man regarded Castells's analysis of the plight of children in today's world as justification, at least in part, for his actions.

As his past appointments in departments of sociology, city and regional planning, European studies, Latin American studies, and other subjects illustrate, Manuel's work also has a wide academic following. Sociology, social policy, political economy, city and regional planning, geography, business and economics, science and technology studies, and politics and international affairs are among the subjects on which he casts an informative light. In each, he has provided new insights which have brought him followers in subjects far from his original academic specialisms.

His intellectual concerns were brought together in the 1990s in the massive trilogy *The information Age*, the foundation of his world fame. This trilogy covers a vast sweep of material. It has a strong interest in identity and social movements, including feminism and environmentalism, the subjects of one of its volumes. Its discussion of technology and innovation, especially the Internet, is an insightful one, based on Manuel's close-grained and continuing work in Silicon Valley and other world centers of advanced technology. It also provides detailed analysis of social transformation in a variety of contexts, especially the collapse of the Soviet Union. And it frequently focuses upon the human condition in many forms. Politics, crime, the nature of work, the status of women and of children, and the collapse of civil society in large areas of Africa all feature in its analysis. By late 2002, the 1,500 pages-long trilogy, of which two volumes were in a second edition, had been reprinted 15 times in English, and translated or was in the process of translation into 20 languages, including Chinese, Arabic, and Parsi.

The Information Age widened the audience for Manuel's work across the world and to many new interest groups. Among those who first encountered him through the trilogy was the present author. I found that the books, although long, were a less forbidding read than many shorter volumes. They also illuminated a wider range of my thinking than many other ambitious works, and – one of the most attractive features of his output – used deep research and evidence to support their conclusions. From my reading of the trilogy sprang an encounter with the rest of Manuel's work and with the man himself, via a range of interviews conducted by email and face to face.

Manuel wrote *The Information Age* after a diagnosis of cancer left him doubtful that he would live to see its critical reception. Its success and his recovery, he says, meant that he could spend as many years talking about the book, in conferences and seminars, as the 15 he took to write it. But this is not the route Manuel has chosen. Instead, his work on new technology has deepened, with the publication of *The Internet Galaxy* in 2001 and, with Pekka Himanen, *The Information Society and the Welfare State: The Finnish Model* in 2002, and his active participation in work on high technology and economic growth in Finland, South Africa, and other countries, mentioned in conversation 2. In addition, his concerns have broadened to include topics as diverse as Muslim Europe and the Russian Far East, an interest owing much to his wife, the Russian Emma Kiselyova.

Manuel's opinions are in demand all around the world. But he is not a consultant or a futurologist. He does work that he finds interesting and that feeds his scholarly and social concerns, not to bring in fees, despite frequent interest from businesses and governments. Most attractively, he does not express opinions about what might happen in the future. Instead, his work is based on tough, empirical analysis of actual events and contains insight rather than speculation. Detailed fieldwork and intense scholarship are the hallmarks of his work. He has been compared to thinkers such as Marx, Hegel, Descartes, and Weber. While he finds such comparisons amusing, Weber is most to his taste because of the immense research that informed his analysis. One of the few ways of annoying Manuel is to compare him to the shoot-from-the-lip futurologists beloved of the business sections of airport bookstalls.

Nor is his analysis merely a matter of theoretical understanding. Instead, Manuel is a political animal whose work illustrates heartfelt concern and sometimes anger: as in these pages, in his answers to questions concerning the exploitation of children and the rich world's neglect of the problems of Africa. At the same time, his appreciation of organizations such as Save the Children and Médécins sans Frontières – that solve real problems in the sometimes hard world he describes – is a human, not a scholarly, one.

Manuel is often skeptical about politicians and their motivations. But he also insists that functioning societies need politicians and other public servants who are capable and not corrupt. He is close to many leading politicians – for example, Fernando Henrique Cardoso, former president of Brazil and an academic collaborator, while in South Africa he is a member (see conversation 2) of a committee chaired by president Thabo Mbeki to steer the technological future of the country and the region.

The scope and scale of Manuel's work might tempt readers of this book to seek in these pages a one-stop guide to *The Information Age* and the rest of his writing. But we hope that it will not be read in this spirit. Instead, it has a number of more progressive aims. One is to develop some areas of his analysis – for example, of political systems – that are not the main focus of his earlier books. Another is to extend his work on the Internet and on technology in general, both because of its inherent interest and because of the rapid rate of change in this area. This book also includes, mainly in conversation 7, his views on the major issues facing different regions of the world, including some not touched on in his other writing. Yet another aim is to give Manuel the opportunity to explain some of the practical consequences of his theoretical work. In this spirit, our approach has been an informal one, involving comment as well as analysis. We hope, too, that conversation 1 – on his life and influences – will be helpful to the many people with an interest in Manuel's work. There is a growing body of scholarly analysis and commentary on his scholarship and his changing interests, with at least three books on his work now in preparation. There is also growing interest in the regional application of his work. A book of debates with Castells on globalization in Latin America will appear in 2003, a companion to the existing volume on his work in the South African context. Readers will also be interested in Manuel's account of his life, and of the influence on him of events such as Paris 1968 and people as diverse as Alain Touraine, Nicos Poulantzas, and Cardoso.

As its title promises, this book is a series of conversations, recorded as they occurred, with a minimum of editing. Most of the book was written in what Manuel has christened "The

Space of Flows," by email. But conversations 5 and 6, on identity and politics respectively, took place in "The Space of Places" – to be precise, Barcelona – in January 2002.

Martin Ince

London
October 2002
martin.ince@britishlibrary.net

Conversation 1

Manuel Castells: Life and Work

MARTIN INCE *Manuel, this is a book about your ideas and your work, focusing on how your thinking has developed, where it has led, and where it is going next. But your life so far has been a remarkable one, which people interested in your work will want to know about in its own right and because of its role in your intellectual development. Please give us the outline.*

MANUEL CASTELLS I was born on 9 February 1942 in a small town of La Mancha, in Spain. The town is Hellin in the province of Albacete. But I have no roots there. My parents were there for a short time because their work was there, then we all left after a year. Since neither I nor the rest of the family knew anyone, I never returned to that town, so my place of birth is misleading if you are interested in my identity. My father (Fernando Castells Adriacnsens) was a finance inspector, and my mother (Josefina Olivan Escartin) an accountant, both civil servants with the Spanish Ministry of Finance.

My father's family supposedly comes from Catalonia, and some traces of it go back to the sixteenth century. But my father and grandfather were born in Valencia. There was a military tradition in the family. My grandfather, whom I never knew, was a high-ranking officer in the Army Corps of Engineers. And so was the eldest son of the eldest son in each generation, until my generation. I recruited my cousin to the clandestine resistance to Franco when he was in the military academy, and he ended up in prison, thus destroying this noble military tradition – his father was immediately discharged from active service. My father was a member of the Phalange Party and fought with the Francoist forces, against the Republic, during the civil war. Later, he became disappointed with Franco, and this limited his promising bureaucratic career. My mother was from a traditional Catholic peasant family from Biescas, a village in the Aragon Pyrenees. She was a very smart, very articulate, very pragmatic woman who was very advanced for her time and context, and always tried to work in her profession. I have only one sister, Irene Castells, two years younger than me. She is a professor of history at the University of Barcelona. I have always adored her, and we have remained very close throughout our lives. Because my father was moving up the career ladder in his finance inspector job, my childhood was spent in Madrid, Cartagena, and Valencia. Finally, I finished secondary school in Barcelona, and I went to the University of Barcelona.

Tell me more about how you view your Catalan identity.

Because I spent the critical years of my adolescence in Barcelona, and because the original matrix of my father's family comes from Barcelona, and because of how I feel, I call myself a Catalan. However, my family was not Catalan-speaking, and Catalan was forbidden in the public realm during the Franco years. But I learned Catalan by myself while I was at the University of Barcelona, mainly for political reasons. I have lost a lot, but I still understand it perfectly and am returning to speaking it fluently. It helps my identity. You could say I am a Catalan nationalist, although certainly not a separatist, and not a supporter of the nationalist party – I usually support the Catalan Socialist Party, which is federalist.

You had a precocious school and college education, I believe?

I entered the university in 1958, when I was 16 (I was two years in advance of the usual age for finishing secondary education). I had always been a very good student, under heavy pressure from my father. I studied at the University of Barcelona, both the "Licenciatura" of Law and the "Licenciatura" of Economics. ("Licenciaturas" in the Spanish system were five years at the university and are the usual degree for anyone not going into an academic career.)

My main thing was literature and theater. I won student and college literary and theater awards. But in the repressive climate of the Franco period, just expressing yourself would get you into trouble with the political police. So, after they closed our journal and censored our plays, I had had enough, and entered the clandestine resistance in 1960, when I was 18 years old. At that time there were only a few clandestine groups active in the anti-Franco opposition at the University of Barcelona. It was a risky activity. One was highly likely to be arrested, tortured, and sent to jail for a number of years, besides being expelled from the university and being blacklisted for any government job. So in 1960, we were probably no more than 50 activists out of 14,000 students. But we were very determined, and very clandestine. The three main groups were the Catalan nationalists, the Communist Party (the main one), and then a *sui generis*, radical group named the Workers Front of Catalonia (FOC in Catalan), naturally with very few workers in its ranks, made up of proponents of all kinds of ideologies, from Catholics to Marxist-Leninists, Social Democrats, and anarchists.

I saw myself basically as an anarchist, although using Marxist theory. I hated the Communists because they were authoritarian and, in my view at that time, they had betrayed the revolution in the Spanish civil war. So, I joined this FOC group, which was very small, but very active (it eventually became one of the components of the Catalan Socialist Party, a part of the Spanish Socialist Party that governed Spain in 1983–96). My life became fully taken up by politics. I still passed my exams, and I read a lot – a lot of history, politics, Marxist and anarchist theory, Third World issues, political economy. I did not imagine myself as an academic. I wanted to be a lawyer, to defend workers and just causes. But I wanted to write. I always wanted to write, and had the hope that after the revolution I would really have the time to write my novels, my poetry, my theater. But in May 1962 we were too successful. In cooperation with other anti-Franco groups, we succeeded in organizing a general strike at the university and in a number of factories, to protest against the government in solidarity with the miners' strike in Asturias. It was one of the major challenges to the dictatorship, and the regime was unnecessarily scared by this small group of basically rich kids with no attachment to the traditional republican parties: it was the new Spanish opposition. So they clubbed us. Most of my friends were arrested, tortured, jailed for several years. I was lucky, and I crossed the border to France clandestinely. I did not have time to finish my studies, and I had no money and no connections.

But you set out for Paris and – in time – for success in academic life.

I headed to Paris. I had an address of a Spanish anarchist construction worker linked to the same resistance group I belonged to in Barcelona. He helped me. I obtained political refugee status, and a very small fellowship for political refugees from the French government. I really needed it because, on top of all this, my 18-year-old fiancée, in a romantic impulse, escaped from her parents' home in Barcelona, joined me in Paris, and naturally we soon had a baby – my only daughter, Nuria Castells. So I enrolled in the Faculty of Law and Economics at the Sorbonne, and finished my degrees in Public Law and Political Economy. I also worked half-time (as an editor in a publishing house) to pay our rent, and shared the care of the child. My fiancée, now wife, was also studying full-time. We divorced six years later, on very friendly terms, and we are still friends. We were simply too young to marry for ever . . . She now lives in Barcelona, and is a very famous demographer. I have always been very close to my daughter. Nuria and I remained – and we remain – very, very close. She is the anchor of my life, the best thing that ever happened to me. She lives in Geneva now, where she is an economist with the United Nations, with her husband and children, and we are in daily contact by email.

I finished my "licence" at the Sorbonne. In the meantime I was disappointed with Spanish politics in Paris exile, so in 1964 I decided that my future would be in an academic career, because it was freer than any other job, and was close to my intellectual and political interests. I decided on sociology because it was the most politically charged discipline, but I had no idea what sociology was. So I asked around who was doing "working class sociology" (it turned out to be called in academic terms the "sociology of work"). It was Alain Touraine, the rising star of French sociology. I went to see him without having any idea who he was. I asked him if it was true that there was something called sociology that could give me a job (and a fellowship to start with) for studying the strategies of class struggle for the working class. He laughed, and said yes. Then I asked if I could do my dissertation with him on the miners' strikes in Asturias, and he said yes again. He later told me that he was seduced by my naiveté and determination. But I was the one who was really seduced by him. Within months I enrolled in the doctoral program with him at the Ecole des Hautes Etudes en Sciences Sociales, the French elite social sciences graduate school in Paris.

Touraine has been very important to you, personally and professionally. Tell me more about his role in your career.

Touraine, a historian by training, was aiming to found a new school of sociological theory, and taught me everything I know, in the fundamental sense. He is extremely cultivated, a great empirical researcher, a most sophisticated theoretician, knew every culture, spoke many languages, including particularly perfect Spanish (his wife was Chilean), had been teaching and researching in America, and was very political, very committed to good causes, but independent from any party's discipline, my kind of socially responsible libertarian.

Touraine became, and he remains, my intellectual father. My entire intellectual life, my career, and my life, were shaped and protected by Touraine. Without him I could never have survived the ideological repression of French academia. (For instance, Pierre Bourdieu tried to destroy me professionally.)

It was only thanks to Touraine that I survived as an academic in the Parisian elite institutions. And Touraine protected me in spite of the fact that in explicit terms I was not his disciple. I went into a Marxist intellectual trajectory, not following his very abstract and sophisticated theoretical paradigm, because I felt the need to communicate to the world of political change through its language – Marxism.

I did my dissertation with Touraine. But not the one I wanted. Instead, I accidentally became an urban sociologist. Touraine got a big research contract for his center from the regional government of Paris to do a most boring study: a statistical analysis of patterns of industrial location in the metropolitan area of Paris. He had no interest in it, but his center needed the money. So he needed a tough research assistant to do it. Unlike most sociology students in France at the time, I had some notion of statistics. And Touraine was always worried about how I could survive on my tiny fellowship, me a poor political exile with a young wife and a baby. So he was thrilled to offer me a well-paid job as a researcher at his center, with the chance of using all these data for my dissertation, and finish it quickly. Besides, there was not much urban sociology in France at the time, and this could be an expanding field (it was). Yet I said no. This seemed to me like a plot to lure me into the capitalist technocracy and into this bourgeois field of urban sociology. So I said no, and no, and no. Until Touraine felt he had to fulfill his paternal duties, and offered me a stark choice: either the shining path towards being a premier theorist in urban sociology, and in the meantime getting out of poverty with a good salary, or he would drop me from his supervision, my doctoral enrollment would be in jeopardy, and I could lose my meager fellowship.

This is how I became an urban sociologist. Of course, I finished my dissertation quickly. It was based on a statistical analysis of locational strategies of industrial firms in the Paris area – I did discover the specific pattern for location of high-technology firms, so for the first time understanding the logic of high-tech companies. And then in January 1967 (I was 24) I was appointed (again by Touraine) assistant professor of sociology at the new Nanterre campus of the University of Paris. This was a dream sociology department: the professors were Alain Touraine, Henri Lefebvre, Michel Crozier, and Fernando Henrique Cardoso (later president of Brazil – this is how we have been friends since 1967).

One thing everyone seems to know about you is the fact that you were involved in the tumultuous events of May '68 in Paris.

Even more interesting than the professors was the student movement that started to develop on this campus, centered in the sociology department. Among my first students was Daniel Cohn-Bendit, who went on to be the leader of the May '68 movement and is now a leading Green politician in Germany and Europe in general. So, politics again. While working hard on urban sociology, discussing Marxist theory in the seminar of the philosopher Louis Althusser at the elite Ecole Normale Superieure, and teaching methodology (I knew how to count, unlike most of the French philosophers who had converted to sociology), I entered fully into the semi-anarchist May '68 movement. It started on the new Nanterre campus where I was working. The May '68 movement was an extraordinary experience, one of the most beautiful of my life. Suddenly, revolution was possible, was there. But not the political revolution, not the seizure of state power, but the change of life, of being, of feeling, without political intermediation. These were two exhilarating months of nonstop intellectual/political debate, demonstrations, the self-management of everything, and free love. Naturally, at the end, political realities clamped down, and the political revolution was crushed. But not the ideas, not the ideals, that went on to change our way of thinking, and therefore, through many mediations, our societies. Not only France, but the world at large.

But the story ends in another political exile.

I was caught by the police in one of the demonstrations at the end of the movement, by mid-June 1968, and expelled to Geneva. It was the first flight of my life – courtesy of the French government.

I landed in Geneva with no money and no job, with a two-week permit. The correspondent of *Le Monde* in Geneva, Isabelle Vichiniak, took me into her home. Then Touraine helped out, and Unesco gave me a six-month contract to teach methodology in Chile. This is how I discovered Chile, in 1968, and became attached to that country. Although I could not stay more than six months then, later on I managed to obtain a visiting chair at the Catholic University of Chile, so using the hemispheric difference. Between 1970 and 1973 I taught in the French winter in Paris, and in the Chilean winter in Chile. This is how I participated in the Allende experience of democratic socialism in Chile, while teaching, researching, and writing – until the 1973 Pinochet *coup* barred me from access to Chile: my third exile.

And the fourth not far away, I think?

At the end of my first Chilean experience, in November 1968, my friend Fernando Henrique Cardoso invited me to his home in São Paulo and asked me to become a junior professor with him in Brazil, the country of the future. I said yes, and I was ready to become a Brazilian, but before we could implement the project, the military intervened in the university and expelled Cardoso and all the leading Brazilian intellectuals: this was my fourth, symbolic exile.

Time to try somewhere a little more stable?

In 1969, exiled from Spain and expelled from France, I ended up in Montreal, where Touraine's connections offered me a regular academic job at the University of Montreal. I loved it. I fell in love with Quebec. Yet, politics in Quebec was dominated (justifiably) by Québécois nationalism. I could not fully inject myself into that project, although it had all my sympathies. Then, in 1970, Touraine convinced the French Government to pardon me, and offered me a new job as associate professor with tenure at the Ecole des Hautes Etudes en Sciences Sociales in Paris, again using my methodological edge to organize the methodological training program for doctoral students in all areas of study. I finally organized a doctoral program in urban sociology. It established me in the French (and international) academic world.

But presumably you continued to think politically at the same time?

I went seriously into Marxist theory in the 1970s. My entry point was not Althusser, as people think, but Nicos Poulantzas, a Greek political philosopher who studied in Heidelberg and Paris, and became the most sophisticated and most political of the Althusserian group of philosophers in Paris, becoming a professor at the University of Paris. He was one of the most famous political theorists in the world in the 1970s. We entered a deep intellectual dialogue, and became very close friends, almost brothers. His suicide in 1979 was one of the most devastating experiences of my life.

My attempt to bring together Marxist theory, urban sociology, a Tourainian knack for social movements, and my personal emphasis on empirical research led to the writing of my first book, *The Urban Question*, published in French in February 1972. For me it was simply to put my thoughts in order, kind of my notebook of thoughts and projects to work on urban sociology from a new, more political perspective. It became an instant hit in France and in the world (10 translations, dozens of editions, well over 100,000 copies sold in the world of a most abstract, theoretical, academic book, usually obscurely translated, specially in English). However, together with Lefebvre, this became the foundation stone of the so-called New School of Urban Sociology. It took over the academic world of urban studies for the next decade.

Tell me about the attractions of the US academic system – which is about to become your so-far permanent academic base.

While working on my urban research in Paris, I was increasingly attracted by American universities. I admired the institutions, their flexibility, their seriousness, the quality of their students. And I was much more "American" than "French" in my style of research, always interested in empirical inquiry, then adding a French theoretical touch, and a Spanish political angle. So, I seized the opportunity to become a visiting professor at the University of Wisconsin–Madison in 1975 and 1977, at the University of California–Santa Cruz, in 1977, and at Boston University, in 1976, while keeping my professorship in Paris. Then Spanish politics called me back. Franco died; Spain was on the verge of becoming a democracy. Urban social movements were rampant in Madrid and Barcelona, and they were using my writings. So in 1977–9 I lived between Paris and Madrid, helping out the development of urban social movements, while investigating them. Then, in 1979, Spain was a democracy, the municipalities of the main cities were in the hands of the Socialists, my friends were in power, my theories had been vindicated, and Paris was boring and stagnant. I was wondering about my life.

   Then out of the blue came an offer from Berkeley to take an urban sociology professorship. Why not? Why not try to the end the academic project, now that Spain was free, and Paris was beyond hope of doing anything intellectually significant? This is how, in September 1979, when I was 37, I became a Berkeley professor. In Berkeley I started by immersing myself in research on the city, to know the place, and to feel the society. The city means San Francisco, since Berkeley was and is a village – and an unusual one, beyond my comprehension. So I studied urban social movements in

San Francisco, the Latino movement, and I discovered the gay community and its capacity to transform cities, politics, and culture. I brought together all my 12 years of work on urban social movements around the world in my book *The City and the Grassroots*, which for me remains my best urban book and the best piece of empirical research I have been able to do. It received the 1983 C. Wright Mills Award, one of the most prestigious in America. But it was not as influential as *The Urban Question* – because I clearly departed from Marxism, so my ideological followers were disappointed, even if I made explicit that I was not anti-Marxist, just that I could not use Marxism any longer as a tool to explain what I observed and researched.

Most readers of this book are waiting to hear about the origins of The Information Age: *can I feel it coming on?*

In 1983, having finished my decade-long research project on urban social movements, I was thinking about what next. It came to me, without me having to find a subject. Silicon Valley, right next door, was exploding with technological ingenuity, business innovation, and cultural change. I sensed something big was happening, much bigger than we thought in Europe. So I decided to work on the relationship between technology, economy, and society.

But I took two precautions. First, I would run an initial test, analyzing this interaction on a field of study I knew well: cities, regions, spatial transformation. This led, six years later, to another big book, *The Informational City*, that opened up a new field of research in urban studies, calling attention to information technology and its spatial consequences. Second, I would start from California, but I did not want to fall into the ethnocentric approach characteristic of Daniel Bell's post-industrialism theory, the main theory on the matter at that time. I was helped by the fact that my Socialist friends came into government in Spain in 1983, so I spent time in Spain, advising and researching – although never working for the government, always from the university world. I spent one year in Spain in 1984–5, directing a major study on the social and economic effects of new technologies at the university, but sponsored by Prime Minister Felipe Gonzalez's office. A two-volume book was published in 1986 with a preface by Gonzalez. Thus, I was measuring, and analyzing, the techno-social transformation simultaneously from California and from Spain. I went on in 1988–93 to split my time between Berkeley and Madrid, where I created an Institute for the Sociology of New Technologies at the Universidad Autónoma of Madrid.

In the meantime, I decided that to avoid ethnocentric biases in my big project, I had to know more of the world, and particularly the Asian Pacific, the seedbed of new development. I accepted visiting professorships at the universities of Hong Kong and Singapore (I wrote a book comparing the two cities' economic development), and lectured and researched in Taiwan, South Korea, China, and Japan – with a few excursions to other Asian countries. And I still kept in close contact with Latin America, particularly with Mexico and Brazil. Then, in 1989, when the Berlin Wall fell and the Soviet Union opened up, I went in depth into understanding this process of change, and retrospectively the Soviet Union in its reality. This decision was helped by the fact that on my first visit to the Soviet Union in 1984 – in Siberia, invited by the Academy of Sciences – I met Emma Kiselyova (then director of international relations at the Institute of Economics), who came to Berkeley in 1993, and became my wife, after a long and complicated process. So, between 1989 and 1993 I conducted a number of studies on the Russian transition, in cooperation with Russian colleagues, in Moscow and Siberia. Emma Kiselyova and I wrote a little book, published in 1995: *The Collapse of Soviet Communism: A View from the Information Society*, summarizing these studies.

In 1993, I decided to leave Madrid completely, go back to Berkeley, and concentrate on organizing, elaborating, and writing the book that I had had in my mind for 10 years – but at a slow pace, anticipating maybe another 10 years of further research and elaboration, from the protected environment of the Berkeley campus. Emma decided to join me at that time. We started a new life. And then, in August 1993, after a few days of being back in Berkeley, I was diagnosed with kidney cancer.

With Emma's full support, I confronted the illness. They removed one kidney, and thought that the result of the operation was good. There is essentially no effective treatment for kidney cancer except surgery. So, after the operation I talked to my surgeon and told him I had something important to do, and I needed to plan my time accordingly. "How much time can I count on, for sure?" He answered: "For sure, three years." So I organized myself to write the book I had had in mind for so long in these three years – while still teaching full-time in Berkeley, because this was my job and my salary. My wife Emma helped very much. The book became a trilogy, *The Information Age*, even trying to compress as much as I could. There was too much information, too many ideas, and the topic was evolving in real time, particularly the Internet and the process of globalization.

By the summer of 1996 I thought things were under control, I felt physically very well, so I gave myself an additional three months to finish the trilogy. Well, exactly three years after my operation they discovered a recurrence, which led to a a much bigger operation – I shall spare you the details. I organized myself to print an unfinished trilogy. Yet, I survived, and the operation was a stunning success – I got the best surgeon, the one reserved as the last resort in these cases. So, one month after leaving the hospital, I was up and running to finish my book. When I was almost done, my wife fell gravely ill, and needed major surgery as well. I almost gave up, but she convinced me I should go on and finish this project that we had done together. I sent the final volume of the trilogy to John Davey, my Blackwell's Maecenas and protector, the day before I took Emma to the surgery, in February 1997. She also had successful surgery and is doing very well now.

And then another life-altering event: the appearance of The Information Age?

After I finished the trilogy, and Emma left hospital, we took a sabbatical in Barcelona. Then I was stunned by the extraordinary, immediate impact of the trilogy around the world. Between the publication of the first volume in English in November 1996 and early 2002, it has been reprinted 15 times – including a 2000 edition that features a 40 percent new first volume and a substantially revised third volume. It has been translated, or is in the process of being translated, in time order into Spanish, French, Chinese, Swedish, Portuguese, Russian, Bulgarian, Croatian, Turkish, Korean, Japanese, German, Italian, Romanian, Danish, Parsi, and Arabic. In all the languages in which it has been published until now it has become an instant hit, with multiple reprintings. So I decided that for the time remaining to me I should engage in a dialogue with people around the world – academics, grassroots groups, political leaders, and the business world. They all wanted to talk to me. I had to be very selective: I receive about 1,000 invitations per year at the moment, but decline 85 percent. And remember, I teach full-time in Berkeley, and I care very much about having time with my wife, friends, and family. I relate to the world in two ways: the media – through interviews, mainly by email, but also face to face when I find myself somewhere. Second, by organizing tours of specific areas twice a year, using the summer vacation and the Christmas vacation, and always traveling with my wife. So we go to Europe every year (Spain, England, France, Russia, and lately to Finland and Sweden), and in 1998 we went to Argentina and Bolivia, in 1999 to Brazil and Chile, and in 2000 to South Africa. Seminars, debates, learning from the experience, providing my views, and going beyond the analysis presented in the trilogy. In the meantime, Oxford University Press seduced me into writing a little book on the Internet, *The Internet Galaxy*. But for me even a little book is a lot of work – research, thinking, writing. It took me two and a half years and was finished in April 2001 and published that October.

Tell me about the life you lead now in Berkeley [in 2001].

After my second operation in October 1996, I set myself on a temporary horizon, living from six months to six months, the span of my medical examinations. I was not being anxious or thinking about illness, just living in the present, not thinking about anything else – and I was not nervous or depressed. I was very happy to see that my work was creating the debate I always wanted. Then, in 2000, my doctors told me they thought I was over the danger of recurrence. I did not and still do not believe them really; but since I feel great, and since examinations are now only once a year, the time horizon has gone back.

As for my family, I am lucky to be married to the love of my life, Emma. Not many people can say that, particularly when you meet your love in Siberia, in the midst of the Soviet era. I have a daughter, Nuria, with a wonderful husband; she is an economist, and he a cutting edge computer scientist (recently featured by the BBC for his work on the brain's neural networks relating to computers), and two magnificent grandchildren, Clara and Gabriel, who live in Geneva. I also have a wonderful stepdaughter Lena, and her daughter Alexandra, whom I consider my granddaughter. I am very, very close to the two of them, and we often spend vacations together (they live in Novosibirsk . . .).

I live in Berkeley in the same house that I bought (with help from the university) when I arrived here in 1979. I work about 10 hours a day, mainly from my study at home, a lot on-line. I have no secretary, no research assistant, no special treatment (I teach like everybody else at Berkeley, six hours a week). I have been very well treated by the university, and I am at the very top of the professorship ladder, but without any kind of privileges. I am an individual artisan of research. But I do receive huge amounts of information from my students (always duly cited), who are excellent, and from many people around the world who have sent me their work for information and comment.

I love Barcelona, and so does Emma. Maybe – who knows? – we will end our life there. In any case, I want my ashes to end up in the Mediterranean, in front of the Barcelona beach.

Conversation 2

Innovation
New technology: the internet, biotechnology and even nanotechnology

MARTIN INCE *Most of these questions arise from your Internet Galaxy book. However, they relate mainly to the Internet as it affects business and work. Many other questions on the Internet will also arise when I ask you about the cultural, community, and intellectual effects of new technology during other conversations in our collaboration.*

In this conversation – which will be long, but is absolutely central to the public appreciation of your work – we shall also go into biotechnology, nanotechnology, and other areas of innovation. But the Internet is the core of your work and will account for most of the space.

You point out that in the past, networks were personal things, while central control and hierarchy were the way power was organized – political or business power principally. But have there not always been knowledge workers, many fewer than we have today, whose skill was in knowing people rather than in knowing things?

MANUEL CASTELLS Certainly. Personal networks were always a factor in the process of elite formation. But they remained, by and large, personal. It is because they were personal that they were able to create a cultural glue, and a complicity with other persons in power positions. What I refer to is the fact that the institutions of society were built primarily around vertical hierarchies, such as states, armies, churches, built around command and control systems, centralized, and able to mobilize resources on the basis of discipline and direct control. So some personal networks at the top would use these centralized, hierarchical organizations to impose their interests and values on the rest of society – and could be countered only by similar kinds of vertical organizations, such as rebel armies or revolutionary parties.

In any case, all kinds of historical distinctions have to be made, to help to contrast the analysis of the emerging social structure, not as absolute evidence. I do not think we have enough evidence to build a fully-fledged historical comparison. At any rate, the key distinction now is that we are not just organized around networks, but around information technology-powered networks, able to manage complexity, and to coordinate functions and perform tasks with networks of any size and complexity.

The question everyone asks, but here it is: are we seeing something new in the net, or a vast growth of something long established?

Frankly, the question of newness, which I am asked again and again, is a boring one, and I would say not very productive. I think it is obvious that global electronic communication from many to many, in real time or in chosen time, is a new technology, and a new organizational form – indeed, a new medium of communication. But ultimately, I do not care if it is new. It is our essential medium of communication, around which most dominant activities, and a growing share of our personal communication, are being structured. Thus, we must take it seriously, and investigate it, and consider its specific effects, as we did with the whole set of industrial technologies. I think the relevance of your point is to cast a healthy doubt on all the bombastic claims from futurologists and techno-prophets, of the kind that states, "We have the Internet, so everything changes." Of course, society is a complicated system, full of causal interactions, that shape and twist technology to unexpected uses. So it is correct not to infer a total transformation just because there is a new technology of communication, however revolutionary, as the Internet is. But to be cautious vis-à-vis the ideological claims of technological determinism should not lead us to the easy way out, of seeing society as fundamentally unchanged because there is nothing new under the sun.

You develop at length the argument that the web and the net in general were needed for the transition to a new and more flexible society, and that the web is now the basic machine that carries the world's economic, political, social, and cultural traffic. But you add that the Internet is a highly concentrated machine. Most of the users are in the most highly developed parts of the developed world. And, from the supply side, the most used web sites are too. Indeed, New York, San Francisco/Silicon Valley, Los Angeles, and two other cities house 381 of the top 1,000 web sites. While the San Francisco area has been altered completely by the IT industry, the other main centers of web activity are places which were economically dominant for most of the twentieth century.

A number of questions arise from this. First, is this "economic geography as usual," with people clustering near universities and venture capital in the way my family once clustered near the docks of the Mersey and the coal deposits of Yorkshire?

There are indeed many and important questions arising from this apparent paradox that you point out very well. First, the fact that a structure is flexible and decentralized in its working does not imply that there are no nodes. On the contrary, a network is based on nodes and their interconnections. The key issue is that these nodes may reconfigure themselves according to new tasks and goals, and that they may grow or diminish in importance depending on the knowledge and information that they win or lose. The relationship between the flexibility of the network structure and its spatial configuration is an open question, that must be settled by research, not by supposedly common sense. In my book *The Informational City*, published in 1989, I analyzed, on the basis of empirical observation of trends in the United States, the emergence of what I called "the space of flows" – that is, the formation of trans-territorial complexes of activities, such as financial spaces or media production spaces or high-technology world chains of production, made of specific places that were connected with other places throughout the planet, but largely independent from their immediate surroundings.

The Internet accentuates this phenomenon. We observe that the ability to reach out to the planet from a few locations concentrates the core centers, the producers of innovation, and the knowledge elites. In this sense, yes, the production of the Internet and of Internet content reproduces the logic of industrial districts of your family's industrial past. Except that this time, the resources are not coal and steel, but knowledge and entrepreneurialism.

Why are most new jobs in cities? Is it because knowledge workers like to think that other knowledge workers are nearby even if they never meet them? In the UK, and I believe other countries, many large organizations (banks, government departments) have shifted apparently routine bureaucracy out of city centers to save money, or for political or electoral reasons, to spread employment into areas with too few jobs. Will this cost such organizations their creative and competitive edge?

On this matter, we have ample empirical evidence. Companies cluster the innovation, design, knowledge production and high-level management functions, and decentralize routine operations and the distribution of goods and services throughout the country and throughout the world. It is concentration and decentralization at the same time, precisely because high-speed information technologies allow the formation of this scattered pattern while keeping the concentration of the core.

Remember, instead of seeing the end of cities as the techno-futurologists were claiming, we are experiencing the largest wave of urbanization in human history. As of 2002, over 50 percent of the planet's population is in urban areas.

And current reliable projection's indicate that by 2030 about two-thirds of the population will be in urban areas. South America is already 80 percent urban – in contrast to the popular images of Latin American peasantry as the dominant culture.

Of course, this is not the result of the Internet, but mainly of the destruction of traditional agriculture, the lack of services in rural areas, and, as a result, massive migration to the magnets of wealth creation in every country: the metropolitan areas. These metropolitan areas are increasingly interlinked by high-speed transportation, forming megacities that then link up with each other across the planet, by air and sea links. Information technology is critical for the formation of this global transportation system. The Internet makes possible the circulation of information and the generation of knowledge in the whole planet on the basis of what happens in a few centers of innovation and management.

Why is innovation territorially concentrated? Well, on this matter we also have a 20-year-old record of research and theory, regarding the structure and dynamics of what Peter Hall and I labeled "milieux of innovation." Peter in his great book *Cities in Civilization* (1998) has provided detailed empirical analysis of the decisive role of major cities throughout history in cultural creativity and technological innovation. This is why Picasso had to go to Paris, and all major film directors and actors had to go to Hollywood, and all key innovators in electronics and software had to relate to Silicon Valley, and writers in English (and often in other languages) had to be in London or New York, and why major scientists have to cluster in the key academic centers of the world – and the reason why American universities have the lion's share of Nobel prize winners, often born in other countries. There is a social network of interaction, and a set of values, and a set of institutions and organizations that create the conditions for synergy – the source of innovation, of creativity, and of productivity. Because this knowledge and creativity create wealth, this wealth is spatially concentrated, and offers greater possibilities of personal advancement and social well-being. So the overall trend is major spatial concentration of value, and control and absorption of all other places in these generators of value, precisely by the use of the net.

Might it be true that the net can transform isolated areas despite this argument? Even a simple web connection multiplies the information and work prospects of a rural house far more than it would an urban one with libraries and universities nearby.

Here is where common sense does not work. In all countries, including the USA and Western Europe, let alone developing countries, the diffusion of the net in rural areas is way behind that in urban areas, and the highest concentration of net users is in the largest cities. There are, however, deliberate policies that use the net to prevent the depopulation of rural areas (for example, Finland, as we shall see below), as well as for the distribution of education and health in remote areas (for example, Brazil). But overall, the logic of the net is not one of dispersal but of networking, reflecting the dominance of economic functions and social elites.

The same uneven distribution of web access applies across the world, including China. Does the proliferation of the web open up a means of cultural integration between East Asia and the rest of the world that has been elusive in the postwar era, or will cultural and language differences continue to make this difficult?

Culturally speaking, the web has a double effect. On the one hand, it creates global networks of contact and exchange, in English. This contributes to the formation of global, cosmopolitan cultures, including cosmopolitan countercultures, such as hackers. On the other hand, cultural identity finds its full expression in the Internet. While English is still the predominant language, its share of web pages is in decline. In 1999–2000 in Europe the two languages growing fastest on the web were Dutch and Catalan. Because of its flexibility, the web is at the same time the expression of global exchange and of specific cultures. As for East Asia, English is still understood by only a tiny minority of the population there. So what we observe is that in 2000, South Korea and Japan had the highest ratio in the world of own-language web sites to English-language ones. So, for people at large, I think this could strengthen their cultural identity rather than dissolving it in the new globalism.

In the web world you discuss, someone in Paris is more likely to be in contact with someone in Los Angeles than with someone in rural France, especially in the context of work. (Here you use the, to my eyes hideous, term "Glocal.") But although Paris is a world city, if you live there, you cannot help being part of Paris. How do people have a divided life with one foot in Paris and one in cyberspace?

Cyberspace is not a place. It is a corridor between places. You live in your place, and then you circulate in cyberspace, meeting people who live in other places. However, you can also use cyberspace to be in your mental universe. This is what we are doing now [during the course of this email interaction]. So, cyberspace is a hyperspace, a space of the mind, that you practice every day, meeting people and thoughts from other places and from other times.

Also on the cyber lifestyle, you point out that technology has made it possible for people to work nonstop and for their employers to find them wherever they are. There are some jobs where people expect this pressure, but in most they do not. At the same time, some employers are realizing that what they term the work/life balance is neglected at a destructive cost to businesses as well as people. Do you think that the employers who realize this will win out against the ones who extract every milligram from their personnel? Will poorer workers be sweated in call centers while professionals make their own hours?

In fact, the issue here is not about employers but about people themselves. When I write about 65 hours a week as the average working time of a Silicon Valley engineer, this is what they really want. True, they are also expected to do this, but if they are self-employed, they work even more. People who are not part of this drive – let's say semi-skilled workers – are disposable and replaceable from the employer's point of view. So, for the employer, the consideration is to extract work, not to improve their life quality – except if morality intervenes. This is why, with the acceleration of the work process, workers' defense continues to be a fundamental issue: they cannot count on their employers. The problem is that the individualization of management/worker relationships makes the use of traditional forms of defense, in terms of collective bargaining and trade union–led struggles, very difficult except in the public sector. Unions are realizing this and finding new forms of pressure, sometimes in the form of consumer boycotts to press for social justice and human rights. Also, individual explosions of violence by defenseless workers could be considered forms of resistance.

Next, a few more questions on business issues. Why are there so few successful pure on-line businesses? The exception we all know is Amazon, but even that is far from being profitable at the time of writing [early 2002]. And is the idea of what you call "financing on the basis of expectation" really so new? Examples of long-term speculative investment from the eras of railways or canals onwards might be cited.

Pure on-line businesses could not be successful in a world where most people made little use of the Internet, and where the security of financial information is far from assured. Furthermore, there are very few pure on-line businesses, except those selling information. Amazon, and many other e-commerce businesses, rely on a vast system of storage and transportation. There is a lot of click and mortar in e-business. Exceptions are financial services, which are profitable, and some genius initiatives, particularly the auction system invented by eBay. But there was too much hype around B2C [business to consumer] e-commerce when the real transformation underway was, and is, the transformation of all kinds of business by using the Internet, always integrated into the entire realm of a business. Again and again: the Internet is not something separate from life as it is, but a key communication tool that revamps our world while keeping it in its physical and social dimension.

As for financing on the basis of expectation, you are right, this is certainly not new. It is found in all periods of historical innovation. So, in a sense, the new economy is new in relationship to the mature economy, not so much by comparison with the periods of frantic technological and business innovation.

More interesting, I think, is the use of the net by existing companies. Many of the changes you describe got going before the Internet did – the cutback of inventories, the operational rather than commercial merger between firms and their suppliers. But in the web era there is a network that supports all this at a higher level. Do you agree that these changes are also dependent on changes in old-economy infrastructure (such as motorways that are used as warehouses) and political relations – the reduced power of trade unions to disrupt industrial activities which are always in a metastable condition on the edge of collapse?

All this is there, and it is all interrelated. The key point is the historical sequence, and the relationships of causality. Socioeconomic restructuring came first. The network enterprise preceded the widespread use of the Internet in business. And the transformation of trade unions, and of industrial relations, resulted from the emergence of the network enterprise, the shift to high technology and service activities (new activities, scarcely unionized), and globalization. But all this new socioeconomic system (based on globalization and the network enterprise) could expand and blossom because of the possibility of using the Internet, a technology that was dormant for one quarter of a century before being fully appropriated by business and by society. Because technologies are used when a use is found for them, not earlier.

Although (may I say?) you often write about the net in a way that might almost be thought of as anthropomorphizing it, you are clear that it is human effort that creates value and profit. And the people who generate most are the ones who can navigate the vast world data sea. Is your suggestion that share options offer them something akin to anarchist control of their organizations a serious one, or perhaps a piece of Catalan humor?

Human work is always at the source of everything in the economy. But how this work creates value, how it is organized, how it is distributed, is not constant. The intelligent and strenuous effort of farmers in Mexico for the whole year cannot compete in value creation in our economy with one hour of cutting edge software programming for the mobile Internet in Helsinki. Now, if people share substantially in the capital of their company, and they control their means of production (essentially meaning their minds in most high-technology industries), this is self-management. The issue remains that many other workers in the company do not have this control either of capital or of the means of production, because they are executants, and they need the machines they are given to execute, and also that there is a hierarchy of management (but increasingly flat). But overall, a case can be made about many high-tech companies as a form of temperate self-management. Certainly this is the case for small start-ups.

In any case how much control do people with stock options have? They may become rich or stay comparatively poor, but do they have a genuine say in what their employers do?

They do have some say in the most innovative companies. They are encouraged to do so. Companies depend on feedback from their most talented employees. But it is true that decision making at the top is still highly personal – indeed, leadership is more important than ever in a fast-track business environment. But self-management was never in contradiction with decisive leadership.

Finally on work, a parochial British question. The UK has low unemployment [at the time of writing in 2002] and a bad shortage of skilled people. It also has policies towards immigrants that come close to racism – indeed, a principal reason for British fears about EU expansion has to do with the possibility of more immigration. But in the USA, skilled immigrants are welcomed in many cities (although not unskilled ones). Why the difference when the UK has had recent mass immigration that has been so beneficial?

This is one of the two most important differences between the UK (and the rest of Western Europe for that matter) and the USA in terms of their differential ability to prosper in the new techno-economic paradigm. The other is the superior quality of US research universities – only Cambridge is comparable in the whole of Europe.

The openness of the US to immigration (mainly to high-skilled immigration, but in fact to immigration in general) is the decisive advantage. The USA prospers by absorbing over 200,000 highly skilled new immigrants per year. In Silicon Valley, in the 1990s, 30 percent of the new high-tech companies created during the decade had a CEO who was either Chinese or Indian. Add many others of other nationalities, and the share of foreign-born innovation is substantial. Given the bad quality of the US primary and secondary public schools, it is safe to attribute a large part of the success of US technology and new economy to the immigrant input.

Why not in Britain? Racism and xenophobia are the obvious answers. Why more than in the USA? Because the USA was an immigrant society from the start, so the culture and the institutions were open to immigration. Of course, the USA is racist, and particularly racist with one of the oldest American ethnic groups, African Americans. But America has tackled the issue of racism up front, while Europe persists in the illusion that European societies are ethnically homogeneous, save for a few immigrants. Europe is multicultural and multiethnic, and because of the differential birthrate it will be increasingly so, not only because immigration will increase, but because of the current, large, ethnic minority populations. But the public culture, and many politicians, hide this fact, and try to appease the fears of the mainstream. As a result, there is no social basis for letting immigrants in on a large scale, although Britain is moving faster than the other countries in opening the door to the necessary skills. The other reason is that unemployment in some areas of the country, and for the least skilled people, is still a problem, and unemployment feeds racism and xenophobia in all situations. The immigration issue is critical in Europe, and in the UK, both as a decisive input into the new economy and as a permanent feature of the new society.

One possible explanation is that immigrants are needed because of the high growth caused by the United States being transformed by the Internet. Do you think that a permanent gap is opening up here? Or is it more like the postwar period when the USA accounted for half of world trade, a position it was bound to lose as other economies were rebuilt?

No script is pre-written. The new economy, based on the Internet, is global. The USA started first, because of its superior innovative capacity in technology and business, but the new economy is global. Europe and the rest of the world are increasingly structured around new economy practices. The issue is that if institutions outside the USA are not willing to fit into the new economy, the gap will increase. Immigration policy is a fundamental flaw in European competitiveness, and the inability to accept and manage multiculturalism a fundamental flaw in European society, parallel to the inability of the USA to alleviate poverty. But the world is increasingly networked, so competition is no longer between nations, but between firms and between individuals. So the real issue is: which are the territories where valuable nodes of global networks of wealth and knowledge tend to build their conducive environments? They are primarily US metro areas; but a few other nodes have emerged in Europe, particularly London, Stockholm, Helsinki, Copenhagen, and

Paris. Germany is way behind, as it is somewhat paralyzed by the logic of the industrial era. And while Madrid, Barcelona, and Lisbon are emerging, they are still underdeveloped in terms of human capital and money.

You point out that many very human interests have turned into money – everything from securitized environmental programs to, in effect, countries, because of their debts. At the same time most money has become very intangible and moves about the globe at net speed. Does this mean that the risk of such programs or countries crashing is bigger and has gone beyond human ability to prevent? Is there a way of drawing back from such risk, or will we have to get used to it?

The risk is greater, in spite of the ability of markets to correct themselves at high speed. But there is no way to control global financial markets, and since global financial markets condition monetary policies and interest rates, we have lost control of national economic policies. Interventions are always possible, but within the parameters dictated by the movements of global financial flows.

And perhaps a word about the customers whom all this e-business is aimed at. Many of them find the on-line experience frustrating. Are they often the real victims of new systems which have been slimmed down in personnel terms but are over-complex for the end user?

Yes, it is unnecessarily complex, and much of the problem lies in the quasi-monopoly of Microsoft over the end-user operating systems and applications. However, as a new generation comes up, having been born and educated in the new technological environment, and as Linux-based software, network technologies, and other open source technologies develop, the use of the net will become fully accessible. The issue is not so much the technical skill but the social, educational, and cultural capacity to know which information we need and what to do with it. As for users of my generation, we should befriend our grandchildren to be able to obtain their guidance and support for us to fade from the new technological environment in a smooth, humane way.

Next, let's try to use your work in different countries to get a better analytical grip on innovation issues than one gets from the many observers who are over-influenced by the example of Silicon Valley. Here we shall use your recent work on Finland and South Africa, as well as your earlier thinking (especially with Peter Hall) on technopoles. European governments are especially prone to attempts to imitate California – partly because of its success, I think, and partly because of the hold of the United States over economic and cultural thinking around the world. At the risk of reinforcing this hegemony, let's start with your work on Silicon Valley, and let's abbreviate a large amount of careful research almost to the point of destruction. First, shall we agree that the image of Silicon Valley as the product of raw private enterprise is a false one?

Yes, Silicon Valley is an extraordinary combination of elements, of which business entrepreneurialism is only one. And this is not a small matter, since it is the seedbed of the information technology revolution. Historically speaking, an institutional actor, Stanford University, was absolutely critical to starting up the process, with the foundation of the Stanford Industrial Park in 1951. And this initiative came from the personal initiative of Frederick Terman, the provost and former dean of engineering at Stanford. Also, military research funding and military markets were essential to create the semiconductors industry in the 1950s and 1960s, although from the 1970s onwards military markets came to represent less than 20 percent of total sales of Silicon Valley (Los Angeles was much more dominated by military markets, and much less innovation came from there). Thirdly, the hacker culture from all kinds of origins, including students, university researchers, and all kinds of alternative types in the Bay Area, was essential in the personal computer revolution, and later on in the Internet revolution.

Fourthly, the migration to Palo Alto of William Shockley, the inventor of the transistor, in the mid-1950s, was essential as a source of knowledge at the origin of the semiconductor industry, and this was purely fortuitous. But one can also argue that the frontier culture of the Bay Area was a major source of innovation. For instance, Shockley had tried to commercialize his invention on the East Coast, and ATT and RCA were not interested, dependent as they were on vacuum tube technology. The same thing would happen again with ATT in 1970, when it rejected the free transfer of Arpanet [the predecessor of the Internet] from the Defense Department, simply because it had a vested interest in analog-based communications technology. The Bay Area has always been prone to think the unthinkable, and to dare. So there is indeed an entrepreneurial layer, but this is more in the culture and institutions of the region than in the actual business dynamics. It is an openness to new businesses rather than a business culture. Later on, in the 1990s, the openness of the Bay Area to immigrants from all over the world was crucial to attracting the talent, and to building the global networks of innovation, on which Silicon Valley is based nowadays.

To the red-in-tooth-and-claw American, it is obvious that insecurity incentivizes people, while to Europeans it is equally clear that high-wire performance is encouraged by the presence of a safety net. In Silicon Valley, did the sheer amount of opportunity create a work culture in which skilled people did not think unemployment was a concept that they need consider?

In Silicon Valley, individuals took their chances. They did not think unemployment. They thought opportunity. They expected nothing from the state. They despised government. They still do, except to get protection against terrorists. Government, in general, is the enemy, particularly for the entrepreneurs, and for undocumented immigrants is the danger. The libertarian culture is an essential ingredient of the innovation system in Silicon Valley. On average, a start-up fails seven times before succeeding. The issue is that the safety net is people's ability to use their skills and their education to get good jobs while recharging themselves for the new project. Of course, there are also many personal failures, and most Silicon Valley engineers have very tense lives, and very miserable personal lives, with a high incidence of isolation, depression, drug and alcohol abuse, and a high suicide rate, besides the usual story of broken families, although this is a general trend in the USA and is not specific to Silicon Valley. Some studies from Santa Clara University have shown a much greater individualism and more selfish attitudes in Silicon Valley than in the USA at large. Now, state funding was not given to people, but was made available to companies that induced spin-offs that ultimately reached the entrepreneurs. And funding of university research from the Defense Department was a critical element in forming the hacker culture. These were military-funded hackers.

Silicon Valley has a distinct and highly developed pond of capital and some equally specialist capitalists to invest it. Mainly on behalf of clients at a safe distance, they traded high returns on some investments for total losses on others. Is it true to say that funds like this were especially available in Silicon Valley? Has this model for encouraging new businesses been more successful than the (for example, Japanese) route of innovation via subsidiaries of large corporations?

Venture capital in Northern California has been absolutely essential in fostering high-tech companies, entrepreneurialism, and innovation in Silicon Valley, and thus in spurring the information technology revolution. An outstanding Berkeley doctoral dissertation by my student Matthew Zook, finished in 2001, provides empirical evidence for this statement. About a third of total venture capital in the USA was concentrated in the San Francisco Bay Area. These venture capital firms often came from the high-tech industry itself, with good insider knowledge of the next new thing. In all cases, venture capitalists worked very closely with their start-ups, monitoring their development and advising. Venture capital is the heart of the innovation system in the new economy. This is hardly imaginable in a corporate, top-down structure à la Japanese, always with long-range objectives fixed by government technocrats, rather than relying, as venture capital and start-ups do, on a flexible organization that reacts to trends in technology and in the market as they arise, and builds high risk/high reward business projects. Of course many fail (about 40 percent of them in Silicon Valley), but even failures are full of lessons, and the overall outcome is a continuing burst of innovation. This is the real source of superiority for Silicon Valley and for the American new economy at large.

You are emphatic about the importance of higher education as a provider of people and ideas in the Silicon Valley story. I think that for a non-US audience the way this works is one of the hardest pieces of the picture to see. Europeans in particular have no concept of universities having large amounts of cash independent of the state. In the UK, Oxford and Cambridge have such money, but they are the exception. In Silicon Valley, Stanford has long been a magnet for entrepreneurial faculty who like being paid properly and for students with entrepreneurial as well as technical ambition. In later life they tend to turn into big donors, using the US system of socialism for the rich in the shape of tax breaks for donations. Do you feel there is any point in trying to re-create this pattern elsewhere in the world, or is it too distinctive to the USA?

The other source of US structural superiority is the American research university system – let's say about 50 out of the more than 4,000 universities and colleges in the USA. This is really essential, because it draws some of the best talent from all over the world. Remember that about 50 percent of Ph.D.s in science and engineering in America are foreigners, and many of them stay in the USA, where they can better develop their abilities. US superpower status largely derives from this university superiority, because it translates into absolute technological leadership, not just in military applications, but in most areas. This has to do with the institutional system, and most importantly, with the absence of a national ministry of education supervising and deciding what to do.

But the key is not the public or private character of the university. Berkeley and the other University of California campuses, or Michigan, or Wisconsin, or Texas–Austin, are public universities, and are still major research institutions, at the level of the best private universities. Furthermore, MIT or Harvard, as well as Stanford, receive more public money than private money. Yes, donations from alumni help, and the private endowments of Princeton (the largest), Yale, or Harvard, are sources of university power; but they mainly help the nice life of faculty and students, they are not really a differential factor in research and innovation. Princeton and Yale are way behind Berkeley and UCLA in research, in spite of their much greater wealth. Yes, governments and corporations do provide more money to the research universities than they do in Europe, but the reason is that these universities are indeed very productive and very useful. Their flexibility, their autonomy, their decentralized management, the cooperation between faculty and graduate students in the graduate programs, their intellectual openness, their resistance to endogamy, their competitive environment, and their uncompromising commitment to academic values and excellence over anything else enable them, generally speaking, as sources of knowledge and innovation. If, in addition, you have a university as entrepreneurial as Stanford (unlike Berkeley, which is more enclosed in traditional academic values and distant from the business world), then you have a natural and synergistic relationship between university-, business-, and government-funded programs. That is at the root of Silicon Valley.

Is this extrapolable to other countries? Yes and no. In principle I do not see the reason why institutional reform could not proceed. The university I am at at this point in Catalonia, the Open University of Catalonia, is publicly funded, privately managed, has private contributions, still keeps academic values, is flexible, is virtual, and works very well. But it is a new university founded by an entrepreneurial rector with strong support from the government of Catalonia. In most countries – Europe, but even more Japan – government bureaucracies and corporatist interests in the academic world, plus demagogic attitudes among the students, block any attempt to open up the university. Thus, students dutifully perform their tasks for so-so degrees in their countries, and then the wealthiest or the most entrepreneurial go to the American university system to get the real thing. I am convinced that the most important imbalance between the USA and the rest of the world is in the university system, the source of knowledge and education, and thus of wealth and power, in the information age.

Finally on Silicon Valley, it seems to be the place where business met up with Californian counterculture in the form of the hacker mind-set. By this I mean not so much the desire to sit up all night and eat junk food while trying to read other people's private files, as the wish to understand computer systems and networks, share this understanding socially, and innovate on an informal basis. People who do this exist everywhere, but why is Silicon Valley a unique machine for turning their expertise into business?

Countercultural types and hackers are critical sources of innovation, because they innovate for the sake of innovation, for their pleasure, for their use value. Then some get rich out of it, others become famous, others drop out, others go on with very normal lives, but all are made happy by creating and innovating. Therefore, they provide the unexpected openings that the system (economic, institutional) cannot generate by itself.

The California culture, even more so than US culture at large, and the university culture are full of these types, plus the libertarian individualist ideology of doing it by myself and for myself. Thus, it is a milieu of innovation, where there are maximum possibilities for hackerism to happen, hackerism in the Himanen sense, the passion to create, regardless of the uses of the creation. The transfer from this to business proceeds through the entrepreneurial culture and institutions, through the flexibility of the labor market, and, more fundamentally, thanks to the existence of well-developed, well-managed venture capital networks. This is what the Valley is all about.

Do you know a book called Cyberselfish *by Paulina Borsook? It is about the far right views of many of the denizens of Silicon Valley. She seems to have written it as an antidote to the idea that there is anything public-spirited about their informal and apparently benign ways of doing business.*

Yes, I know the book, and I do not like it. It is a very angry pamphlet, and nobody ever said that the Silicon Valley entrepreneurs were social types. They are indeed profoundly individualistic, but selfishness is a different matter; some are, some are not. The main flaw, though, is that she assimilates entrepreneurs and hackers or innovators into a single type, and this is profoundly wrong.

Some of your work on Silicon Valley has been done with the Finn you just mentioned, Pekka Himanen, who lives there. With him you have also done work on the new economy in Finland itself, supported by groups including the state innovation body Sitra. I think that the report you produced teaches many deep lessons. For one thing, it dispels the Silicon Valley myth that technological ingenuity requires orange groves and sunshine.

Finland is exceptionally interesting because, as we show in our book (with Himanen), it was a poor periphery of Europe 50 years ago, and is now, according to the United Nations Development Programme, the number one information society and, according to the World Economic Forum ranking, the most competitive economy in the world. In our book we show that Nokia is the core of an information and communications technology sector that is itself the core of the new Finnish economy, but there are 3,000 firms in this ICT sector, of which only 300 work for Nokia, while working also for other firms. Finland is a leading country for what are now called electronic manufacturing services (meaning subcontracted manufacturing), a key segment, because it is where production quality and the learning curve are located. But the largest Finnish/Swedish bank is also the leading financial institution in electronic banking in the world, and there are many examples of small and medium firms that are innovative and competitive. Tampere is becoming a major design and production center for e-social services, the most important frontier of development for the network society and economy at this point.

People who think about Finland and IT think of two things – Linux, the unix-like operating system for Windows-haters, and Nokia, the mobile phone firm. Of these, the second is more significant, as you say, and is also a startling story that will yield MBA case studies for many years to come. The firm was completely reinvented as a mobile phone company after getting into severe trouble as an old-style conglomerate. The decision to sell everything except one minor subsidiary and build it up worked well. But you add that Nokia is not the whole story, and many other smaller firms are involved in both equipment (broadly defined) and content. Is this because the cultural factors that allowed Nokia to succeed in its new form were present for others too?

It is far more than Nokia, but Nokia remains a major force in Finland, and in the world, and this is only the beginning. When the third generation of mobile phones and full Internet access come of age, we may really enter the mobile network society, and Nokia will benefit greatly from this development. (Ericsson and Motorola have difficulty in following its pace of business innovation, while in fact being better at engineering.) Nokia is using its growing power to extract concessions from the Finnish government, particularly to lower taxation and increase immigration quotas for its engineers. Indeed, there is increasing tension between Nokia and the Finnish government, and talk about Nokia leaving Finland. It is possible that it will move its headquarters out of Finland, as Ericsson did from Sweden. But this will not destroy the Finnish economy. Nokia's major research and development units are and will remain in Finland, intimately connected to excellent engineering and scientific schools that the government has created. And because there has been enough technological diffusion in Finland that most of the country, and particularly the Helsinki/Espoo/Vanta/ Tampere region, together with Oulu in the north and Turku in the west, is now a major hub of technological innovation, engaged in a constant search for new products and new services. The major threat to Finnish technological growth is not the flight of a few Nokia offices, but the declining interest of Finnish youth in science and technology.

Is something else they have in common the fact that they both have higher education institutions which place a high emphasis on science and engineering and that in both, graduates take a relaxed view of the future and do not feel the need to get a routine job with a big corporation as soon as they leave college?

This is why my Finnish friend and colleague, Himanen, thinks that social hackerism and cultural innovation could be the next round of innovation for Finland, socially responsible, and also with potentially huge markets in the world at large. Because, although Linus Torvalds [the originator of Linux] now lives in Silicon Valley, the Finnish university system that nurtured him and many others like him continues to develop. By the way, the Finnish university experience shows the possibility of creating a very good university system in a few years (Finland went from three universities in 1967 to 20 today). The Helsinki University of Technology is now among the top five European universities, and in the leading pack at the world level. They combined a top-down approach, with government money and support, with an opening up to international networks, and with close cooperation with companies, but respect for the rules of engagement, so that university researchers keep their autonomy. No, not all is perfect in Finland, besides the weather and the xenophobia, which are bad; but there are many lessons to be learned for those who would not like to become like Silicon Valley in order to innovate.

This leads us to what Himanen calls "the hacker ethic" and, more importantly, the way in which Finnish society has, you say, provided enough safety nets to let people take chances without starving or freezing. Is there a large element of chance about the process that turns such opportunities into success?

The main lesson is that the welfare state not only is not an obstacle, but can be a critical provider of well-taken-care-of human beings, who are, after all, the main source of innovation.

Is it partly because Finland was a network society even before the network was electronic – the organizations fit together properly and each has its own role and status, the different actors respect each other and everyone knows who is responsible for what?

No, Finland was not a network society, and still is not in many areas and in many institutions. Particularly, the welfare state and government administrations are highly bureaucratic, and this is the contradiction emerging between a network society in the core business sector and among the professional elite, and the protected sector relying on old rules of social organization. The problem is how to dynamize this sector while preserving the welfare state that, as I said, is critical in the Finnish mode, since Finland does not have the resources of military programs or of major corporations, as was the case in the USA. Sitra [State technology agency] was crucial in providing venture capital and guidance to several initiatives and many firms (including Nokia) at critical moments. It had the intelligence to substitute for the missing private venture capitalists while managing programs, in most cases, with an entrepreneurial spirit.

Perhaps the strongest match between the Finnish and Silicon Valley models is that in both, some sort of critical mass of different actors was necessary to get an innovation culture working. Educated people, a system for financing their ideas, a structure to allow them to talk to each other, were all necessary. In Finland and California, areas with technical universities turned into nodes for internal migration. By contrast, Silicon Alley, the web-innovation hub of New York, did not have a big engineering center nearby, and as a result has been more of a small-scale design center feeding on the New York media industry. But in all three cases, the societies in question are, like Japan, very future-focused. In the case of Finland, survival and independence were issues of importance in recent times, and Finland's close economic links with the Soviet Union meant severe trouble when the USSR broke up. Now Finland is the world model of a mobile information society. Does this make it easier for other big challenges in the country's future to be faced?

Your comparison between Finland and California is very insightful. Yes, a critical mass of non-business actors was essential in triggering the innovation process (universities, federal funding, countercultural innovators in California; government initiative, public venture capitalists, universities, welfare state in Finland). Migration, though, is different. It was essential in California, both internal and international. In Finland, there is little international migration (this is a weak point of the Finnish model), and internal migration to the south was proceeding anyway by the depopulation of the peripheral regions. In Finland, the interesting point is that the government used high-tech development and new universities to fix the population in the northern areas of the country, or in rural areas that would otherwise have been entirely depopulated. This is how Oulu, Rovaniemi, Jyvaskyla, or Lappeenranta became technological innovation milieus in a few years. Education in this sense was essential in both places, but in Finland was home-grown and in California (where the public school system is of very bad quality nowadays) proceeded through immigration of the best talent from around the world.

New York also benefits from immigration (40 percent of New Yorkers now are foreign-born), and in fact there is a great deal of innovation in New York in areas of what I would call tech culture and tech media, besides, of course, the fundamental role of financial innovation. The future? Yes, Finland, like Japan, is obsessed with the future. I guess it is the culture of survival, the culture of nations and people that experienced the real possibility of being swallowed by other cultures and nations, and reacted – or overreacted, like Japanese imperialism. California, I am less sure. It is entrepreneurial, it is frontier, but it is more focused on the present, certainly without a past (no sense of history), but probably also without thinking too much about the future, since the notion is that the future is being made in California, so the future is what Californians do, and will become the future for the rest of the world. It is also in a certain sense a culture of survival, but of individual survival, the survival of the immigrant, while Finland or Japan want to survive together, as a culture, trying not to be invaded by the outside world.

The common factors which such apparently diverse societies as Finland and California share also point up, for me, the sheer size of the problem faced by another country, South Africa, which you have studied. In The Information Age, *Africa appears largely as a continent with many horrific problems, and we revisit them in this book in conversation 6. The work you have done there, with the approval of President Mbeki and the participation of many academics, executives, and others, suggests that even the enthusiasm of such powerful actors will not prevent many South Africans remaining in the Fourth World.*

You are right about South Africa. I think Mbeki is a sincere, honest, very capable leader, in spite of his strange uncertainties about the HIV virus, which have been so costly for him in terms of his image in the world. I know he is convinced that while the Internet cannot be eaten, countries cannot eat without the Internet, in a global, networked, information economy. Thence, the strategy to develop ICT and the human resources to handle it and to use it, in South Africa first, later on in Africa. I am convinced that this is an essential project, and I accepted being a part of his advisory council, together with leaders of the major ICT companies in the world (with the fortunate exception of Microsoft). I must say I was pleasantly surprised by the energy and availability of these leaders, particularly Carly Fiorina [head of Hewlett Packard], to engage in this project. And yet, the task is so overwhelming, resources so scarce, coordination and implementation matters so complex to solve, that by the time something will happen, South Africa and Africa will be in an even deeper level of economic decline and social deterioration. I do not think we can proceed in such a slow, orderly manner. The world is revolting and disintegrating at the same time.

You point to crime, drugs, human trafficking, mass emigration of skilled people and other problems which South Africa has in abundance – plus, of course, HIV/Aids on a tragic scale. In the same report, Stephen Gelb points out that the state and the market both form part of the network. But is it true that in South Africa, as elsewhere, the state is the key actor without which everything else will not work and that civil machinery that works – in other words, which delivers services, is not too greedy or corrupt, and which gives other actors confidence – is the key resource?

We need thinking, yes, but we know enough for governments, business, civil society, social actors, to act, and to act quickly in engaging a new shared, global model of development. I fear the consequences of failing this urgency. As for what to do, in general terms it is relatively simple. I presented it in my address to the Economic and Social Council of the UN in May 2000, and I repeated it at the first meeting of the newly constituted UN ICT Task Force in New York in February 2002. Besides the investment in telecom infrastructure adequate to the needs of developing countries (meaning satellite-based and access by mobile telephony to a large extent, plus open source software with specifically developed applications), there are two key issues. The first is education, particularly of teachers. Since there is no time to proceed in the traditional way, this means mass, virtual education based on the Internet. We have the technology, we have the e-learning experience, and there are large institutions (for example, the University of South Africa, where Mandela studied) that could be retooled to go from their traditional role as distance education institutions to the new technological medium. Second, the Internet is not a gadget, but a tool. So the key is to develop and diffuse specific Internet-based models for agricultural development, for international, high value-added tourism, for preventive health care, for education, for adult literacy, for citizen information and participation, for community-based security strategies, for horizontal communication, and for the diffusion of information, as well as for the diffusion and eventual commercialization of art and cultural creativity. Of course, all this has to be specific to each context and to each country. But the problem is not so much what to do (we know enough to start experimenting) as who does it, for whom, how to do it, and with which resources. So, higher education is the priority, but, as for the Internet, it has to be integrated into a broader strategy of development, otherwise we will simply be producing the next generation of Silicon Valley engineers.

Next, I would like to follow up our IT discussion with a look at some newer technologies, notably biotechnology. When we spoke in Oxford [in June 2000], you said that as an experimental social scientist, you had not written at length about biotechnology, because the biotechnology revolution had not happened yet for you to observe. But I think that the work you have done on one very important technological revolution ought to allow you to articulate some opinions on such revolutions in general, so here goes.

By the biotechnology revolution I mean our ability to get and act on systematic knowledge of how life works. Such knowledge – for example, having the human genome and those of other species available and knowing what they mean – obviously involves huge computing and telecommunications resources. Using this information involves a number of technologies, especially the ability to move genes between individuals and between species. There is already a biotechnology industry, in two forms. One is embedded in older companies, especially in the pharmaceutical industry. The other involves newer firms, often established on the back of a single idea, patent, or discov-

ery. Is there a general rule, on the basis of what has happened in IT, about which of these is likely to be the more successful model?

We observe a very different business pattern between the electronics industry and the biotech industry. In the biotech industry, start-up firms are almost invariably absorbed by large firms, or else very quickly become very large firms with important financial backing. It looks as if the kind of resources necessary to handle clinical trials and the legal and administrative matters is so large that only major firms can really proceed with development, once the scientific breakthroughs are there. This may bias the biotech industry towards primarily market-driven genetic applications, particularly in regenerative medicine and sophisticated medication for grave illnesses. The libertarian strand of Internet innovation seems to have much greater difficulty in making progress in biotech. Biotech is shaping up as a corporate field, very unpopular with public opinion, and under strong suspicion from the regulatory bodies. On the other hand, when your daughter is in danger, you are ready to try anything. . . .

I note that many of the investors in the smaller firms are people from the US west coast (Bill Gates of Microsoft, Larry Ellison of Oracle, Steve Jobs of Apple) who have made fortunes in the IT revolution. Indeed, fierce competitors in IT seem to invest as colleagues in biotechnology. The same applies to some non-US capitalists such as Sir Chris Evans in Cambridge, England. Would the connections in terms of people, money, and technology suggest that the IT and biotechnology revolutions would be best viewed as a single phenomenon?

In fact, I believe that from a historical perspective, both revolutions will be one, the revolution in information technology. After all, genetic engineering (the heart of biotech) is about decoding and recombining the information codes of living matter. There are multiple connections between the two science and technology fields in information processing. This goes beyond business arrangements. It is clear that cash-rich electronics entrepreneurs are taking stakes in what they see as the most fundamental technological revolution, the one that affects and shapes life directly.

But there is more to it. The human genome map could not have been completed without massive computing power. The new frontier of microelectronics is working on genetic material, and electric current is being replaced by chemical reactions. So DNA-based chips are very much in the making. Bio-electronic sensors are the core of nanotechnology, and they are getting ready to go into the body to perform all kinds of operations, while communicating with computer networks with the proper information to make medical decisions in real time. All this is in progress in the research centers I know at Berkeley, at Stanford, at UCLA, at MIT, and I assume in Cambridge [England] as well. There is an even more fundamental convergence between the two technological revolutions: the network organization and its analogies in the human mind. The most important discovery of the human genome project is that we have many fewer genes than was thought, about 30,000, so not many more than the fly, and almost the same as the monkey. The difference seems to be in the networking and recombining capacity of our cells, and particularly the brain cells, through myriads of electrochemical connections. It seems that the logic of emergent properties through layers of complexity on the basis of networking and feedback loops is similar in the Internet and in our brain-controlled life system. My friend and colleague Fritjof Capra is finishing a major book on exactly this, on the convergence of the networking paradigm in nature and society, at the heart of the epistemological breakthrough associated with the so-called complexity approach. I do not like the media hype on the matter, but I believe there is something important emerging there.

Electronics is the same everywhere, but the web is not. In the same spirit, what happens when biotechnology interacts with different social and economic systems? This is obviously an unanswerably huge question, so let me break it down. European countries and Japan mainly have health care systems which are

*paid for by taxation and are free or cheap to the user. In the
USA, profit-making health providers are the general rule. Does
this put the USA at a disadvantage in innovations which require
large populations to give informed consent to data gathering?*

No, it is the opposite. Japan is somewhat different, but in the
case of the European Union, the protection of privacy is so
much more comprehensive than in the USA, and the restrictions on biotech research are such, that probably most of the
European scientific discoveries will end up being developed
in the USA. And because, as you say, profit-making health
care is the norm in the USA, this is likely to bias the great
biological revolution in market terms. The difficult illnesses
of the affluent population, particularly of the ageing population, will receive priority over the simple diseases that kill
millions of children in poor countries. The biological revolution is being captured by the commercialization of health
care and by the structure of global inequality.

*Does it mean, however, that US systems are more likely to adopt
new solutions first because people wanting to make profits are
more energetic than public servants? Or is the litigation culture
of the USA too big a deterrent when some new processes are
bound to be detrimental?*

Again, the litigation culture is less of a deterrent to biotech
than the very strong administrative controls in Europe. The
discoveries do not depend on profit making, but on scientific
passion, as with the hackers in the Internet world. What
depends on profit and entrepreneurialism is the commercialization and diffusion of the discovery, and in this the USA
is the privileged area, yet with a profit-making bias. On the
other hand, the USA may have restrictions in terms of religion, particularly with a Republican administration, since
Christian fundamentalists of different sorts account for about
25 percent of the Republican electorate. The 2001 prohibition of public funding of research carried out on stem cells
obtained from human fetuses is a clear sign of this trend.

*As you say, there are powerful cultural forces arrayed against
biotechnology on the grounds of its interference with fundamental aspects of our humanity. How do battles of unequals
like this get resolved? On the one side, big companies, big
money, big politics; on the other, less formal and less well-
funded bodies which make use of new communications technology and can articulate widespread and deeply held opinions.
One parallel is nuclear power, where it turned out that the out-
siders were right.*

The ethical and religious debate on the biotech revolution
is the fundamental one. There is widespread resistance to its
implications, from different quarters. I doubt that the biology
revolution will proceed as smoothly as the microelectron-
ics/Internet revolution. But the debates are different in the
different dimensions of the revolution. First, agro-biotech-
nology is in deep trouble in the developed world. People are
reacting, sometimes with serious reasons, against genetically
modified food. And the arrogance of business (for example,
Monsanto) has clearly provoked an overreaction. Yet, on
the other hand, major developing countries, such as China or
Brazil, are seeing in this technology a new green revolution,
enabling them to feed their population. In medical research,
the cloning debate has polarized public opinion, missing
the key matter: the ability to clone organs and the promise
of regenerative medicine – that is, the ability to repair our
ageing organs genetically. Also, the ability to screen genetic
defects and act at the time of birth or earlier. Some of the
discussion is simply uninformed: for instance, the possibility
for everyone to live 100 years – this is science fiction of
the worst taste. Even if we could regenerate our organs, the
connecting links between them could not escape ageing. We
may increase the quality of life alongside longevity (reaching
a good life in our 80s) more by acting on lifestyle than on
genetics. But all informed opinions I know really dismiss this
cataclysmic view of a new humanity of aged people.

    But what is really at stake is the ability to manipulate our
own life. And the differential ability to benefit from it,

depending on wealth and location in an increasingly divided planet. I am observing the emerging debate. For the time being it is too general, too philosophical; but when it becomes specific, it is explosive, and may derail or block the biological revolution, as is already happening with genetically modified food in Europe. Not necessarily a bad thing, but it is clearly driven by emotion rather than knowledge. After all, emotion rules societies rather than science, and this is probably a good thing.

Lastly on this, can I ask about some other technological changes now coming along? One is the arrival of nanotechnology, which must be real because there is a special issue of Scientific American *[September 2001] on it. Here IBM seems to have established itself in a lead position. It overlaps with biotechnology because it operates at a molecular scale, as life does itself, but the applications are partly biomedical and partly to do with engineering and materials science. In general, are we looking at a new era of human technological control over the world, paralleled by new scientific knowledge? If so, are the scholarly and social institutions that now exist adequate to allow these changes to be analyzed and assimilated properly?*

Yes, nanotechnology is the fundamental field of applied research that merges the microelectronics and biotech revolutions and, with the help of new materials, allows the power of information processing to be extended to living matter. Berkeley is very advanced in this, and I marginally cooperate in the social corner of a mega-research program called CITRIS, of which nanotechnology is the center. MIT, Stanford, UCLA, the University of Southern California, UC–San Diego, and others, are working full speed on nanotechnology. As with all major scientific discoveries, scientists think only science when they are in the midst of action. Only after they get their Nobel prizes do they start to elaborate on philosophy, and tour the world preaching morality. A great scientist, before anything else, is bound to push the frontier of knowledge, and this is what they are doing now in nanotechnology, and this is their job.

The issue, the real issue, is how society and public institutions harness scientific discovery without suffocating individual creativity and the freedom of research. On this ground, no, our societies are not culturally or institutionally ready to deal with our extraordinary leap forward in science. Societies oscillate between bureaucratic responses and market-driven applications, between irrational fear and unwarranted techno-optimism. We are very immature in reaching this information age.

Conversation 3

The Space of Flows

MARTIN INCE *The one thing everyone I have told about this book has asked is: what is the Space of Flows? I find this odd, as the idea is one I understand instinctively, but it might be helpful to converge on it rather than attack it directly.*

As you say in The Information Age, *every schoolchild nowadays learns the connection between space and time. In the quantum era we know that mass, length, and time, the fundamentals of all measurement, all arise from the same deep structure of the universe. But you point out that the way we perceive them is a very human matter, and has changed over time. The change has been caused partly by technology – most prominently with the development of clocks in the eighteenth century, which allowed position on the Earth's surface to be measured accurately. But you point out that, as usual, technological determinism is not the whole story. Time systems, devised by people, have had an important role in political reform, as you point out in the case of Russia – and one might add other examples, such as the calendar and clock reforms of Revolutionary France.*

So what is it that flows in the space of flows? Is it correct to say that it is information – either in the form of bits and bytes, or of people, or sometimes in physical form as your work on FedEx package destinations shows?

MANUEL CASTELLS The most difficult concept to grasp of my whole theory is the space of flows. Yet, it is fundamental. I have tried again and again to explain it, to illustrate it, because I believe it is the most direct expression of the technological transformation of our existence. But it is difficult, because it is counter-intuitive. Space is always a mental construction. Not only a cultural construction, but a materially mental construction, because we must place ourselves somewhere. But the space of our lives, of our direct experience, is not the space of the economy, not the space of information, not the space of science, not the space of art – all realms of activity that ultimately frame and influence our lives. Thus, to understand the transformation of space, I rooted myself in a philosophical tradition, that of Leibniz particularly, but also that of the genius theoretical geographer Harold Innis and his analysis of regimes of space and time. Leibniz particularly has a very lucid formulation of the concept of space as the material construction of time simultaneity, which is what brings human practice together in time.

Throughout history in most human practice, simultaneity depended on vicinity, on territorial proximity. Now, what happens when we can do things together in real time, but from very distant locations? There is simultaneity, but the spatial arrangement that allows it is a different one. It is based on telecommunications, computer systems, and the places from where this interaction takes place. This is the space of flows: not just the electronic/telecommunications circuits, but the network of places that are connected around one common, simultaneous social practice via these electronic circuits and their ancillary systems.

Is there also a negative and more political definition, which contrasts the space of flows with its obverse, the space of places? If you are not within the space of flows, are you instead in the Fourth World – excluded from the information and access of elites, unable to get educated or participate in economic life, and quite likely deprived of political and civil rights?

What I observed is that the dominant activities in our societies follow this logic, while most personal interaction, and the construction of human experience outside instrumentality, tend to still be clustered in localities, defining simultaneous social practice in terms of vicinity. Thus, global financial markets and global management services are made of financial places, and their systems of companies, facilities, and telecommunications-linked computers constitute a whole financial system throughout the world. Thus, global cities are not just their business centers (New York or Tokyo), because much of New York and Tokyo is very local. The global city is made of many bits and pieces of cities around the world, including financial centers in the developing world.

You show that although London, New York and Tokyo are the biggest nodes of the space of flows, lesser nodes are also present and can change in importance or be added. Madrid, for instance, has been added because of Spain's integration into the world economy. But is there also significant inertia in the system? You point out that Munich's lead role in German technology owes a lot to decisions taken under the Third Reich. High technology in Scotland began because factories moved there to be out of reach of bombing during the Second World War. Despite the example of Finland (conversation 2), it is rare for unexpected places to join the world technology mainstream. Elites talk mainly to each other: is the Space of Flows partly the modern-day way in which they do so?

The part of New York that is global is a much larger share of New York's space than the global space of La Paz, Bolivia. But La Paz is also part of this global network in its tiny financial and managerial center. So the space of flows is at the same time an abstract concept and also a very material construction that connects places as nodes of networks of instrumentality. These places are not meaningful in themselves, but only as nodes of these networks.

I tried to develop a similar analysis for the space of high-tech manufacturing, for information systems, for the criminal economy, and so on. The network is the message in the space of flows. In addition, this space of dominant activities tends to generate a style of architecture, a certain type of cosmopolitan aesthetics, and a series of facilities that characterize the lifestyles of the global elite. However, my theoretical mistake was to assimilate the practice of the space of flows to the global elites and their instrumental activities, while opposing this to the space of places where most people build their meaning and live their lives. Dominant activities are indeed global (from high-tech manufacturing to financial markets, and from CNN to the drug trade), and so are the elites that thrive as their agents. But the space of flows is materially based on the new technologies of communication. So people of all kinds, wishing to do all kinds of things, can occupy this space of flows and use it for their own purposes.

So is it an oversimplification to say that in these countries of the mind, people who lack the life opportunities to have broad horizons and to be comfortable with ideas and information, and who tend to do low-value work are the inhabitants of the Space of Places, while the Space of Flows is the home of the people who have inner and outer resources to cope with the speed of the information age and the demands it makes on people?

While in the early 1990s the space of flows was mainly the space of dominant activities, in the late 1990s, the space of flows became as contested as the space of places, and in early 2002, the Argentinian revolt against globalization largely used the Internet, and the movement extended throughout the world via Internet-based networks. In 1999 I gave a lecture (later turned into a paper) entitled "Grassrooting the Space of Flows," where I corrected my original analysis of the matter. So what is truly important is that the space of flows coexists with the space of places, and both express contradictory social interests, even if, by and large, dominant activities and global elites tend to use the space of flows as their privileged form of spatial practice, because it is more efficient and enables them to remove their practice from the spatially rooted social and political controls (for example, the World Bank in 2001, setting up an Internet and video conference system to escape from physical meeting places surrounded by protesters).

Conversation 4

Social Movements and Organizations

MARTIN INCE *In your Internet book you describe the pleasure with which you noticed a newspaper headline "New uses of the Internet in Colombia." You naturally hoped that new technology might provide hope for this beleaguered country, for which you care greatly. On reading the article, you were disappointed to find that the "new use" it had in mind was the use of email to deliver ransom demands.*

What do we learn from this? Does it show that new technology tends to be taken up by existing organizations (in this case unpleasant ones), rather than allowing the creation of new ones?

MANUEL CASTELLS No, what it shows is that society, as it is, appropriates technology for its own uses and values. If there are trends towards the creation of new organizations or networks of organizations (for example, the anti-globalization movement), powerful technologies, such as the Internet, will power these new organizations. Or will reengineer the existing ones. The fundamental lesson is that technology *per se* does not do good or bad to societies. But it is not indifferent. First, it enhances existing or potential trends. Second, the Internet does have some specific features, such as greater freedom of communication and global interactivity, which make it ideal for building networks.

You point to studies that show that big Internet users also socialize face to face more than others, use the telephone more, and are in general more active rather than less in social life. This shows that people with education, social skills, money (new technology is cheap but not free), and motivation are best placed to make the most of technical innovations. But does the same apply to organizations, whether we are thinking of commercial, official, or non-profit groups? You cite figures pointing out that many British politicians barely have email addresses, let alone a substantial interactive presence on-line.

I think evidence supports the fact that the more intelligent an organization is, the better it uses the Internet, which, in turn, makes it more intelligent, in a productive spiral or virtuous circle. Your point about British politicians seems to confirm this, rather than contradict it. I think it is fair to assume that, overall, political organizations are among the less intelligent in the world. Besides, interactive technology is only effective if you are really interested in two-way interaction, which does not seem to be the case for most politicians, who prefer well-coached and staged "town hall" meetings when elections approach.

This said, I agree that social movements should be studied and understood in their own right, not just from the point of view of technological transformation. This is what I have always tried to do, and still do. On the other hand, if I write a book on the Internet, I analyze the specific link between the dynamics of social movements, and of specific social movements, and the logic of the Internet. However, the key point is indeed that social movements must be understood in terms of what they say they are, because their banners are what attract people to them and turn others away. It is certain that locality is still important. What is happening is that defensive groups such as immigrants and deprived local communities build their territorial trenches as their primary form of organization. But to go on the offensive, to act on society at large, they tend to use networking and the dissemination of information, and they use the Internet.

Much of your work, back to The City and the Grassroots *(published in 1983), is on social organizations. Those you analyze are, or were, mainly urban movements. Most people will be in cities by 2015, and many will need support in their new surroundings. Will this mean more self-help groups to make up for the failings of state provision? As you say, cities are the focus of all money and power – is this why they generate social movements such as US Black power? Or is the reason more to do with the deprivation they generate during periods of growth? Your work on San Francisco shows that the corporate city, the gay city, and the hippy city can exist alongside each other. Do cities generate social movements because they are inherently more tolerant than the country?*

As of 2002, over 50 percent of the population of the planet is in urban areas, or rather, in large urban expanses that look very different from the compact, dense city of traditional European urbanization. And current reliable projections indicate that by 2030 probably about two-thirds of the population will be in urban areas. In developed countries, the current proportion oscillates between 75 and 90 percent, and even in areas like South America, over 80 percent of the population is already urban. Thus, the distinction between rural and urban has lost relevance. We are an urban planet, and the remaining rural areas are fully integrated into the networks of money, information, media, and functional connections that extend from urban areas into the countryside. Furthermore, the bulk of the urbanization process is taking place in very large metropolitan regions that extend over vast areas that include rural spaces within the metropolitan structure – for example, Greater London and the southeast of England, Paris–Ile de France, the Ranstaad, the Southern California metropolis, the New York–New Jersey region, and even more so in Asia and Latin America. Spatial transformation is an essential dimension of social change.

But much of my work in urban sociology was based on the notion that spatial forms do not directly induce culture or social behavior. It is not because you are in a city that you behave in a certain way. The whole matrix of cultural and social interaction is much more complex, so that social practice, modes of thinking, depend on class, on gender, on culture, on personal experience, including spatial patterning as a form of experience, but largely transcending the simple dichotomy between rural and urban. So what is important about the Zapatistas is not that they are rural, but that they are indigenous people – and in this indigenous culture the relationship to land, to their environment, is fundamental. This is why their demands for self-government and their request to control their land are essential as a definition of the movement. It is an identity-based movement, not a rural movement.

Social movements come in all kinds of formats; they are not necessarily progressive. Also it depends how we define "progressive." It is a matter of personal taste. Many people in Latin America, and some in France, still consider communism to be progressive – an opinion from which I strongly dissent. But communism has been, and still is in Colombia, for instance, a social movement, defined as the collective, purposeful mobilization to change the values and institutions of society. So social movements are not the expression of good versus bad, but a key mechanism through which societies change, towards different goals, towards different institutions.

The key here is to be agnostic about the goodness of society. Good for whom, for what, under which circumstances? There are not good and bad social movements. There are social movements, whose goals, beliefs, and struggles are sources of social change in a process that is not predetermined. History has no direction. History has no other sense than the history we sense; it is not outside us, as it was represented by the liberal ideology of progress or by the Marxist conception of the development of productive forces as the engine of linear human development, with class struggle as the device to overcome the obstacles posed by capitalists and other exploiters to the objectively progressive march towards technological and economic progress. In both ideologies, there is the Hegelian march of reason throughout history that becomes the benchmark against which social movements can be measured. If we reject this ideological vision of history, we are left with social movements as they are, and our personal evaluation of each of them, according to our interests and values – which are, of course, entirely subjective.

Another form of social organization in which you have a strong interest is the Green movement. I have been looking forward to our exchanges on the matter, because I feel it is one area on which we might disagree strongly. I have been involved in British Green politics, especially the movement against nuclear power. From your point of view as a social scientist, Green movements are a social phenomenon arising from people's need to assert themselves against a world that is developing in ways they find hostile. By contrast, my own view is that even if you are right, such movements are a rational response to the fact that humans, having started small about a million years ago, are now sequestering a huge percentage of the Earth's biological activity, altering almost every part of its surface, remixing the genes of its species to their own tastes, altering its climate by releasing carbon into the atmosphere over a few years that was captured over millions of years . . . you get the idea.

The Green movement is not a biological reaction to anything. It is a cultural movement. It emerges from the critique of a model of civilization that does not integrate our relationship to nature into the model of economic growth and technological development. In this sense, it contradicts productivism, the priority given to the development of productive forces, and opposes quality of life to quantity of goods. But it is also a science-based movement. It uses our increasing knowledge of ecosystems to foresee the consequences of human action, and to prevent undesirable consequences.

Most people never see a melting icecap, a whale, or a burning rainforest. So is the Green movement a creation of the media?

It is certainly a media-oriented movement; that is, it acts on people's consciousness by creating events and diffusing information over the media. In fact, all important social movements do the same nowadays, as does politics. The relationship between projects and protests and institutional change goes through the media, as the communication system that links up social projects and public opinion.

What about the shape of such organizations? Greenpeace uses the methods used by multinational corporations (its people fly a lot, send prodigious amounts of email) and has a structure reminiscent of the organizations it opposes. Sometimes it even goes into business with the enemy, as with Greenpeace's UK joint venture with electricity suppliers. By contrast, Friends of the Earth organizes more locally and fights more local issues. Do you think that opposition movements are always likely to take on the shape of the groups they oppose?

There is a great diversity within the Green movement, and in volume 2 of the trilogy, I proposed an analytical typology to explain its diversity and make sense of it. All types, though, relate to the media, and all make alliances of different kinds. Some are very close to the corporate world, since they believe they can influence corporations and make them environmentally friendly. Others are more radical; they go to the roots and oppose any development – in fact, proposing a much more austere mode of economy and lifestyle. But what all Green movements do is to place their grievances and their alternatives in the global context. There is an acute awareness that there is a planetary ecosystem, and that saving the tropical rainforest has direct consequences for people living in England. In other words, the Green movement is the most direct linkage between the local and the global in the proposition of alternative models of society.

The Financial Times *economics commentator Martin Wolf said [on 5 September 2001] that what he terms "anti-globalisation.com" is the "world's most effective Internet-enabled service provider." Is he right?*

The anti-globalization movement is a global anti-global movement, and can only exist because of the Internet and because of the globalization of media. It is a very significant movement. It has already forced a debate, and I know for a fact that governments, international institutions, and major corporations are rethinking the whole world to respond to the criticism. It is not just gimmicks. There is now a profound consciousness that we cannot expect the market and technology to take care of social and ecological issues, and that people all over the world are resisting the economic and social order that is emerging. I consider the anti-globalization movement, in all its extraordinary and even contradictory diversity, as the historical equivalent of the disorderly working-class movement that emerged in early capitalism until it formed itself into the labor movement, and then initiated the process of debate, negotiation, and institutionalization of conflict that gave birth to the modern industrial society. It is that important. Its numbers are not big, but they have imposed a debate, and opinion polls show that while most do not support the movement itself, they feel sympathy for many of the issues it raises.

The echo of the movement is much larger than the movement itself, and so are the consequences in institutions and in the business world. This is the mark of a true social movement.

Is the real difference between the Internet age and the age of the social movements you analyze in The City and the Grassroots *that nowadays the balance between social organization and capital has shifted decisively towards capital? That its speed and flexibility are far greater than those of non-profit movements, whether they be political parties or less formal groups – even those that make the most of new technology?*

No, the balance has not shifted toward capital. It did in the 1990s, the golden age of neoliberal ideology which considered that technology and markets could ignore society and identity. But the anti-globalization movement, as the convergence of many disparate reactions, and then the violent attacks from identity-based terrorist networks, have shown the limits of this narrow conception of society. Capital controls the economy, but not at all societies, and after all, business also lives in society, so substantial reforms must be conducted, and we are in the process of debating these reforms.

In The Information Age *you examine the right-wing militia movement in the USA, seen at its most extreme in the Oklahoma City bombing, and Aum Shinrikyo, the murderous Japanese sect. Do these show that social movements can be malign even when they arise from real social forces?*

In *The City and the Grassroots*, I said two things. One, social movements do change the city, and the world. This is why there are social movements. I could show this was the case. Therefore, it is essential to understand social movements, because they are producers of society, of culture, of space. The second thing was that I thought that they improve the quality of life, and the quality of the city. And some of the movements I studied actually did so. But I have changed in my general approach to their positive contribution to society. Then I was still in the position of having a general sympathy for their goals. Now I am much more circumspect. I know, and I have studied, that some social movements can be very regressive in terms of the values I personally support. But they are social movements. So in this sense I am not more or less optimistic, but I am less naive, and more rigorous.

Conversation 5

Identity

MARTIN INCE *This is a complex topic and one I thought would be best tackled face to face. What do you mean by identity? And how widespread is it as an issue?*

MANUEL CASTELLS I would like to start by acknowledging the critical importance of identity in my work. By "identity" I mean the cultural construction of meaning by a social actor. Such an actor might be social or corporate.

When an individual, asked what they are, says "I am a Christian," "I am a woman," or "I am English," they are telling you their strong self-definition, the meaning that makes sense in their life. People throughout their lives have to adapt to what is around them, and adapt what they are to what people want them to be. For instance, most people work, but for many, work is not the most important thing to them. But for others, work is the thing that makes sense to them and provides meaning to them. That meaning motivates people to do the things appropriate to the group they belong to.

How have these issues changed with the arrival of the information age?

Often in history people have had little autonomy – categories of meaning were given. Religion, especially, was a big given. In the modern age, in a secular society with citizenship and citizens' rights, identity is detached from history, especially in the developed world. In many cases this means that the state produces identity, and national identity is especially important in war and crisis.

In most of the world we see a return to identities rooted in history and ethnicity. These identities are constructed using ideas from history, because most people want an identity with deep roots, not a newly created one. But being a Muslim or a Christian, for example, is not the same as it was in the Middle Ages, even though the belief base of each religion is largely unchanged.

People's ability to create a self-definition is absolutely fundamental to the modern era. My work on it is based on many observations of its importance. When British or American people participate in Muslim fundamentalist armed forces, one sees it in an especially stark form, but there are many other cases – for example, the increased ability of people in Catalonia to describe themselves as "Catalan" as their first identity.

Speaking three weeks into the use of the euro as a 12-nation currency, is there space for a European identity along with the others existing throughout the Continent?

As we develop a European identity, other identities strengthen alongside it, especially national ones. There are also many vital sub-national identities. For example, Basque people have a very strong sense of their Basque identity. This has nothing to do with the violent expression of this identity by a radical fringe of Basque nationalism. It is, rather, the expression of a long history of cultural survival and search for political autonomy, always confronted by a centralized, authoritarian state in Madrid.

It is important to realize that these identities are essential to people and are not fading. They are not primitive: they are part of modernity.

What is the role of elites in creating these identities – nationalist feelings, for example?

There are some social scientists who think that everything is manipulated by elites. But in fact although everything is a social construction, identities are not just rationalizations to serve elite interests. They can be constructed, but they need to be built on history and society if they are to work.

So how and why do types of identity arise?

Analytically this is a hard issue to think about. One thing I have done is to establish that there are three different types of identity. One group includes identities built by an elite as a system for rationalizing its view. Such a legitimizing identity is the French one constructed in and after the French Revolution and involving the French nation as the expression of liberty, secularity, and republicanism. This involved steps such as driving out non-French languages spoken in France and using schools to impose a model of what children should be like. This causes dilemmas long afterwards, such as how Muslim children should be educated in French schools.

More powerful than legitimizing identities are resistance identities, in which basic principles provide a powerful source of identity. A current example is Palestinian identity, that of a marginalized people involved in a God-blessed struggle in which martyrdom has become normal. These strong resistance identities are simple and solid in their workings, and have a lot of force. After all, it is very robust if you can say "Global markets pay no attention to me, but God does."

The problem is that identities of this type exclude people outside the group very strongly. But identities such as Scottish and Catalan, which have been renewed in recent years, are strong without being threatening. So a resistance identity does not have to mean fundamentalism.

The third type is the project identity. These are characterized by being strong and dynamic at the same time. They accept change and project themselves to other groups. For example, someone might decide "I am a Catholic" and decide to make converts by assimilation and otherwise. The African-

American project identity is an especially important one. It is the attempt to build a society that respects cultural differences without discriminating.

Would you regard Creationism as a resistance identity? I see it as something that is very culturally specific, being associated with poor, uneducated white protestants. As [the late] Stephen Jay Gould said, there is no tradition of biblical literalism among Catholics. So you do not get Catholics who think the world is 6,000 years old.

Resistance identities can move in one of two ways. They can close in on themselves and become violent if they have no boundaries, and therefore no bridges of coexistence with other identities – for example, Judaism with relation to the Palestinian identity. But this type of identity is very different from one that wants everyone "to be like me." Islam is a community of believers to begin with, but has ambitions to convert the rest of the world. Christianity, too, has the idea of the infidel, and these identities share the idea of enclosing all mankind.

What about the extreme case we mentioned above, of British or US people, some not from Muslim families, joining Muslim armed forces?

That is an example of a mainly defensive identity, in which an individual gets a source of meaning. Despite Islam's world ambitions, most Islamic fundamentalism does not aim to take over the world. It aims at strengthening the Muslim faith in the Muslim world – for example, by protecting holy sites.

But how, for example, does a white American boy find his life's meaning in this?

People whose life is devoid of meaning will look for and get it. A prime example is the Cambridge Soviet spies [a group of Englishmen who became involved in spying for the Soviet Union in the 1930s and were still active in the 1960s]. They took on a working-class project identity, a valid source of meaning for upper-class Englishmen of that era. Another example from the 1960s is the people who joined the Red Brigades of [West] Germany rather than the mainstream German middle-class life one might have predicted.

Can we try to think about how the communities of meaning you describe have changed in the era of networks of technology, information, and capital?

Seeing how they interact is crucial to understanding the modern world. The first point is that these identities are real, not imagined. Their strength depends on their historical conditions of development, often linked to how strongly they are used as either sources of discrimination or symbols of communal resistance. For example, it is easier to have the identity of an African American than to be a Chinese American nowadays, because Chinese Americans now (unlike a century ago) can have easier ways of individual upward mobility. So the group is less necessary as a community of resistance. Or it is easier to be a Christian Black American than a Mormon Black American, although these do exist.

Also, identities are not roles. Some are only attributes, but others are deep and carry the meaning of life for the people who have them. A woman might say "I'm a mother" or "I'm a basketball player." But if you ask her about her identity and she says first "I am a Christian," that is something fundamental about her, and she cannot have many things in her life of that importance. If you have too many, you have to put them into a hierarchy, and that becomes messy.

Of course, even in Catalonia there are plenty of people, as my current research shows, who will say "I am myself" if you ask them what they are. Everyone is their own accumulation of meaning, and they accumulate it in their own way.

Is this why, if you meet an academic at a party, they never say, "I am a professor"? They always say, "I am a chemist" or "I am an economist."

Yes, the issue is that even people who get their identity from their work choose how to do it. There are plenty of people who do this – for example, in Silicon Valley, as well as in academic life. Academics are usually devoted to the content of their discipline and adhere to the principles of what a chemist, say, or an economist is. Some economists feel obliged to hate sociologists and threaten each other with being reincarnated as one.

You speak of these identities as essentially cultural ones. But aren't they also powerful economic ones?

Yes, this is absolutely critical, as is shown by analyses such as those of Gary Hamilton, Nicole Woolsey, or You-tien Hsing, on the fundamental role of trust in Chinese business networks, constructed on identity. The literature on overseas Chinese business networks shows that their economic activity is very effective and is based on trust, not paper. This network has huge enforcing capacity, like a Mafia without the killing, because exclusion costs you a social identity and also your business and credit. The overseas Chinese also link into mainland China and are a key connection to bureaucracies there. In many parts of China, economic transformation is largely based on their influence, with regional, family, and language links. And of course, the members of these networks are enthusiastic users of network technology.

Another striking economic connection is between India and Silicon Valley, as shown by the research of Berkeley's Anna Lee Saxenian. Specific schools and places of origin produce many of the large number of Indian people who are important in Silicon Valley, and who are now setting up high-technology businesses in India. The political and economic networks to which they belong have shared codes of practice which create trust, a clear manifestation of the economic importance of the power of identity. Another case is the Vietnamese community in the USA, which links back to Vietnam via the Internet and in other ways, and is significant in Vietnamese economic development.

For me this raises the issue of Japanese exceptionalism. Has Japan's postwar emphasis on homogeneity and national identity become a disadvantage in the network era?

Absolutely. The term "Information Society" was invented in Japan in 1967. But now Japan has the least information-oriented society of any advanced economy. It does little fundamental innovation – as soon as any development there reaches the cutting edge, it stops dead.

Japanese identity was essential to support nationalism in the postwar era. Homogeneity worked in that era, and Japanese identity was peaceful and nationalistic at the same time. It worked well in the mass production society. But it has since reached a boundary and is failing, so a new way of doing things has to be disseminated. One problem is that the university system is based on bureaucracy rather than on thinking. Another issue is that Japan is not open to other cultures or to innovation. The example of California shows that immigration from China or India could have solved the problem of slow rates of innovation in Japan. Instead, it has been cut off from the high-skill base that the USA has gained from. In the USA, 50 percent of Ph.D.s in science and technology are awarded to foreign students – the percentage in Japan is tiny.

The lesson is that identity is a strong incentive when it is a state project. But if it becomes exclusionary, it is equally a strong obstacle. As I have said (conversation 3), Finland, a great success story of recent years, is on the edge of repeating the Japanese mistake.

Another type of identity you discuss that is immensely important both politically and intellectually is gender identity. It is about 100 years since women began getting some kind of fair deal in advanced societies. What do you think has happened since?

First, although the beginnings date back that far, full votes and rights took longer to arrive. The reality of the patriarchal family also continued, and still does. In Spain, a modern

European country in every way, dozens of women were killed in domestic violence last year. The depth of patriarchal values and structures is very great. The real transformation was from the 1960s onwards, and that means that ideas of equality have been in the mainstream and being carried through for about 40 years.

The origin of the change is the way in which 1960s ideas of personal freedom gave older feminist thinking more force. In addition, the emergence of the service economy, in which women are decisive, gave them more bargaining power, and the landscape changed for them once they were spending significant amounts of time outside the home.

The history of this is intriguing. When feminists put their ideas to supposedly radical men in the 1960s, the men's reaction was so severe that women had to form their own movements. In Italy they were attacked by Maoist men for demonstrating on their own. I think it is the combination of this political change and the presence of women in the work force that was so powerful.

And since?

The amazing thing is that so many thousands of years of history can be subverted in little more than 30 years. Eighteen-year-old women now take things for granted that were unimaginable a few decades ago in terms of their life opportunities. Some of this has been hard for men, but we deserve it. Women have made heroic efforts to cut through a maze of domination and oppression. Their success is now accepted intellectually, but not always in day-to-day practice.

What do you make of the anti-feminist backlash, or talk of it?

Women are present in many centers of power, especially business and politics (academic life has been much slower). But most of the talk about the backlash against them has been directed at dramatic expressions of feminism, not its day-to-day reality. Women no longer need to fight nonstop.

And just as the working class is not co-opted just because working conditions are better, the same applies to women. No battle is ever won for ever, but society's idea that men are superior to women is gone.

Does this mean that feminism started as a resistance identity and is now a project identity?

To a degree; but women are carriers of values as well. This is what the theoreticians call the feminism of difference rather than of equality. Difference is more interesting, but let's have equality first.

Are we now seeing the transformation that this first, equality revolution brought with it?

The challenge is how to combine equality and difference. Women have a history and a set of values that involves a higher level of sharing than men are accustomed to, and this broader, richer, and more flexible tradition would be a major social transformation if it became general. Women do politics and business in a different way from men, and do things in a more multidimensional way – although you still get tough women who feel obliged to act in the tradition of Victoria or Elizabeth I. I didn't like Margaret Thatcher, but she had a role model effect.

The next stage, I think, involves the transformation of the family. The egalitarian, rather than patriarchal, family is a new invention. We are not there yet, and it is problematic. In Spain, women do five times as much domestic work as men, and oversee 80 percent of children's activities. But the patriarchal family is in crisis – young women are saying, "We will do it this way, or no children." Often the answer is "OK, no children." In the USA especially, no-child or single-person households are growing in numbers. Now we are experimenting with other types of family, which alters human minds and attitudes. Children in these families can be happier, but we need hard data about these developments because the issues are very ideological. We now have the first generation of children in non-patriarchal families, and because this is our first experience of this, we need to see the results and where we go with this system of producing children.

But I am sure that when family and social relations are degendered, it will alter the way they work as a source of meaning for people. In the USA at the moment, the situation is like Marx's "false consciousness." There is a lot said about family values, but nobody has families like the ones you see represented. One effect is that it is all but impossible to find candidates for political office – nobody has the necessary spouse and children to match the required image.

In The Information Age *you focus on a particular group – children – as a key one, both for its own importance and as a symbol of the modern world. Why did you choose them as an example?*

I think there is social progress in the world. The trilogy describes many wonderful things; but these generally valuable changes have many horrible consequences too. One of the most striking of these for me is that everywhere we see children who are in subhuman conditions, hundreds of millions of them. Their condition is one of the most striking contradictions of the modern age and is an outrage too big to rationalize.

This is clearly something that animates you intensely and in a far from theoretical way. Why is it worse than other forms of exploitation?

In the United States alone there are 300,000 child prostitutes – around the world the total is in the millions. Then there is the issue of child poverty, which even in the developed world is made worse by selective birthrates, which mean that poorer families have more children. The effect is that although 13 percent of Americans are in poverty, the figure is 18 percent for children. There is also a lack of serious child care. Advanced societies assume that women look after children at home, but also that they are part of the work force. The result is that there is too little time for child care, which turns into work for immigrants or grandparents, and even they are often replaced by the television. This is absolutely not an argument against women in the work force, by the way, but a critique of men, women, and the whole of society. Some societies are better than others at solving this problem, especially the Nordic societies with a larger public sector and more child care.

So what does this tell us about advanced and developing world societies?

Everyone says children are very important, but society does not take care of them. Human life is often not worth much, and people prey on the weak. And who is weaker than children? Child soldiers, child prostitutes, and child labor: all these things happen because children have no defense and are the easiest to use.

In the developed world, people often consume children, not produce them. They have them to keep themselves happy – instead of solidarity, people feel the need to keep their own needs satisfied. So children are the ultimate consumer good. We don't see them as part of ourselves, collectively or individually: we tend more to see them as one of the things in our life instead of seeing ourselves in our children, which reveals our society at its most self-destructive. In a properly egalitarian society, children would be integrated properly. As it is, their position makes society's failings especially apparent. This touches me, and is a symptom of the costs of the way we do things in our society.

How general is the problem?

In most societies, most children are looked after, and their situation has improved. The contrast is extraordinary when you look at the situation of the children who do not share in this. It is seen at its most extreme in the global trade in children, including prostitutes, maids, and child labor, which involves perhaps 250 million 6–14-year-olds. In some cases, but not all, I would include the world trade in children for adoption in this. In some cases, these children's plight is far worse than that of children sent down mines in the Industrial Revolution, in contrast to the general improvement in society since that era, because of the world market in children. They are cheap, and you can do what you like with them as they are defenseless.

Worse, we know about the problem. Child sex tour catalogues are distributed legally. Regulations exist and are not enforced, which they have to be because in the network, great resources and great destitution are linked, and it is easy to exploit the powerless.

However, none of this is inevitable. It is the dark side of the free market, and it needs ethical regulation. Otherwise you have a world in which everything can be sold everywhere. We also know who the culprits are. India has consistently blocked international efforts to help its children on the grounds that this is a plot to support trade protectionism in the developed world. But sometimes pressure succeeds – for example, with Nike and child labor, where it had to concede because of pressure from consumer groups and trades unions.

There are some heroes in this, such as Unicef, which is fighting attempts to block it by governments which are in favor of human rights until someone asks for them. The treaties to provide them exist, but are rarely enforced. An example is the land mine treaty, which the USA refuses to sign – mines kill more children than disease in the mined countries.

So, if you want to know why I have, generally speaking, a low opinion of governments, the treatment of children is a large part of the answer.

Conversation 6

Politics and Power

MARTIN INCE This discussion is going to be on politics, the biggest subject of all in some ways, but I hope we can avoid things getting too general. When we began our dialogue, you said that politics was "the umpteenth derivative of something else." Did you mean by this that in the network world it is the outcome of processes, rather than a driver of them?

MANUEL CASTELLS That is not true all the time and everywhere, but it is especially true across the world now. Politics used to be a driver of society. After all, politics is the process whereby social groups can take control of government institutions and use them. Politics is not power – power is very different, as the classic distinction between power and influence shows. Influence induces particular behavior, but power tells you "Now you will do this." Power, as many observers have said, is the capacity for violence, even though it exists in many forms, some purely symbolic.

Politics, viewed as the process which forms access to government institutions, is about the ability to influence society in ways that favor some actors over others. The issues are complex, but seem to me to have two fundamental principles. The first is that, in the network society, politics is media politics. The media are not just needed when elections have to be won. They are the background all the time, the public space where power is played out and decided. The other rule is that the art of politics is always at the center. The dynamics of all political systems leads to there being two camps, and the center is where they compete. Each side has got the votes of its own supporters guaranteed, so the fight is for the last 10 percent. This means that parties' traditional positions are always watered down, and politics which is seen to be determined by a single ideology is doomed to lose.

Does this mean that there is no real role for center parties?

They have a role, but it is mainly as support parties for one of the other, bigger parties. They may decide which of the blocs gets in, but they cannot govern. The same is true of Green parties, to whom the concept of support parties, which cannot decide the result in their own right, also applies.

This means that the two-bloc logic of US politics is now being reproduced across Europe, and elsewhere around the world. Under this logic, parties become large coalitions – for example, the Labour Party in Britain. The party is only one part of a coalition of groups which has one key component – a single leading personality. While the ideology and policies of each party are different, when election time comes, the programs and platforms of the parties are very similar, and the main message is the personality of the leader. It says, "Trust me; you haven't read the program."

Is this why the media are so important in determining the outcome?

Yes, because the most important tactic is character assassination and the politics of scandal.

What's new about this?

There has always been corruption and scandal. But now all parties and candidates are subject to attacks. We know that negative publicity is five times as effective as positive when it comes to getting people to switch their votes. This means that the parties and media all need to stockpile ammunition

and need intermediaries to leak it to the media when necessary. Scandals usually result from leaks, not investigative jour-
nalism. Often such material is inaccurate, but the damage is
done by the time it is corrected. Sometimes it is like the
Russian story in which two people are talking about a woman
they know of by rumor: one thinks she is "the woman who
stole the coat," while the other calls her "the woman whose
coat was stolen," but they both know who they mean.

In some cases the practice is more sophisticated. When the
Republicans bombarded Clinton, the voters did not care
because they liked his program. Polls show that the voters
regard all politicians as liars. With Clinton they said, "Yes, but
he's our liar."

So why be a politician? Why do people do this to themselves?

It is a job – indeed, a professional career. If you take the opposite view – that you want to change the world – you won't
last long. Being a professional politician is not the same as
being part of a social movement. What I am saying now
applies to being within the formal political system.

You also have to recall that people hate professional politicians. So people in that career have to appear fresh while
being ruthless. They have to seem like idealists but know how
to put the knife in a rival's back as a daily practice.

Isn't being a politician a very high-risk career?

Yes, but it is also interesting, and you can, despite what I say,
make some difference and achieve changes. It is better in
terms of achievement than an academic career, although it is
much harder work. But the financial rewards are less than in
business unless you are corrupt.

It would also be wrong to think that all politics is the same,
and nothing matters. There is some difference between the
things left and right do.

What is the role of corruption in all this?

You cannot be in politics and be clean. You have to play by the rules to succeed. Some time ago, I was in a closed session of a well-known political party, one of whose leaders said, "Politics is the art of reaching power and keeping it." I said, "What about changing society?," and he agreed that was part of the picture – but as a footnote, not the main concern.

For instance, in Britain, the Conservatives lost their power by believing too much in their ideology: Margaret Thatcher is a fundamentalist and an ultra-nationalist. The comparison is with Spain, where the Conservative Party now has a strong hegemony in a country which is not naturally conservative. They got power because of the exposed corruption of the Socialist Party. This led to general public disgust and a sense of betrayal. So the Conservatives were elected for negative reasons, and they will last until the new Socialist leadership, that replaced the old one, shows they are different.

So does this mean that the life of a political activist is bound to be a frustrating one?

Yes, I would say so. There are very few cases of people active in political parties who think they can achieve change without being professionals. Most activists are pensioners, are actual or would-be professionals, or are Trotskyite infiltrators, although this breed is almost extinct, except in France. Young people involved in politics now are usually there to make a career. There are some exceptions, and one is the US Republican Christians, who often do not hope for a political career and are driven by their religious beliefs.

Is the media intensity of politics something that has been exported worldwide from the USA?

Yes, but the difference is that in US politics, people are very straightforward about it, or cynical if you like. Politics is all about money there, and people know what is needed to run in dollar terms. If you cannot raise millions, you cannot get support. In Europe, things are hidden behind a screen of party apparatus. But in both cases it is a very frustrating exercise and generates cynicism.

Why exactly is this a problem?

The issue is that we do need people to represent us. This means that there have to be processes so that people are accountable and on occasion have to give some favors, which is what I think of as harmless corruption. With some exceptions, the people get cleaner the higher you go – although the high-level entourage of Mitterrand was one very big exception, and there have been media accusations concerning Berlusconi in Italy. It is at the lower levels where the power and resources are produced, and the leaders know this. Most political parties have real substance in the people at the top. But the individuals are always very pragmatic and go with the wind. Good politicians who last have strong realpolitik. Mission-driven politicians tend not to survive.

Do you have any hope of campaign finance reform – for example, current moves in the USA to restrict major donations?

Rules on how politics is financed are all very important. In scandal and media politics, money is the main resource, and who pays is decisive. The current [January 2002] Enron scandal will be remembered in this connection. According to media reports, so many Texan politicians were on Enron's payroll that it was a problem to find judges to hear the case and representatives to investigate it, because they had to confess conflicts of interest. It also embroils the vice-president's campaign, although not the president directly.

Part of the problem has to do with the looseness of the rules, but changing them will be difficult. All attempts so far have been blocked, because politicians have to vote for them. Why would they vote against the machinery that is the basis of their success? It is a contradiction in terms.

How different are things in Europe?

Politicians have freer access to media advertising, especially at election time, which is better, although even in Europe a lot of politics consists of created events. The cost is also less in Europe. But in another way things are worse. Even though European media politics costs less, it is still expensive and is beyond the reach of political parties by open, legal means. The result is that they get money which is offered in the hope of favors when the recipient is in power. The trade-off is simple – "Money today, but think of me next time" – and it works systematically. Sometimes it works at a very high level, as with rumors about the financing of Kohl's party in return for support for abandoning the Deutschmark for the euro. But at all levels the bottom line is that things hidden in Europe are visible in the USA, of which the second is preferable.

The solution is public money for politics, on a national basis. Like judges, politicians need public money so that they can afford not to be corrupt. The problem is that most members of the public hate to give public money to corrupt people and parties, so they have to resort to illegal financing of politics.

There are some exceptions, and one is Singapore. In many ways Singapore is not my favorite country. But paying top public servants there more than the private sector would has cut corruption hugely. So has the existence of an anti-corruption unit with wide powers. The housing minister there, suspected of corruption, committed suicide after a visit from them.

In most places systemic corruption involves decisions in exchange for resources. It is rare for money to go to individual people. Instead, it goes to the political machine and is systemic, not personal.

What do you regard as being the boundaries of political power? For example, is it about the size of the public sector? Or about having a stable system for other actors such as enterprises and individuals, which, as you say, is absent from such places as Russia and much of Africa?

Of these the size of the public sector is probably the most important left/right difference these days. Most people think that bulk nationalization is counterproductive, but also think that the state is an appropriate provider of services, especially health and education. The left favors state provision, but often with some deregulation – in other words, the welfare state – while conservatives favor privatization with some form of regulation. This choice leads to different decisions on taxation, because you cannot have a welfare state on low taxes. But state funding based on taxation is redistributive of wealth. The problem is that polls suggest that people hate taxes and don't trust politicians.

Isn't that a good thing in some ways?

It means there is no solidarity between people, and no trust in politicians. But then if you ask people if they are willing to pay more taxes for free health care, subsidized transport, good education, and the rest, they say yes. People support hypothecated taxes [those earmarked for specific purposes], even though economists hate them. Americans are always amazed at the free or cheap college education which Europeans expect. Saving for it is a fundamental considera-tion for most US families.

Does your work on Finland, a successful technology nation with high taxation [conversation 3] illuminate this?

Yes, Finns support high taxes, and people appreciate what they buy. The services that taxes pay for are appreciated, provide a solid basis for Finns' lives, and give them peace of mind. Besides this, they are the foundation for productivity and competitiveness of the Finnish companies in the global economy.

All around the world, the welfare state is the political defining line. All the evidence is that liberalizing and priva-tizing education and health, especially, costs more and pro-duces lower-quality results, and concentrates resources at the top of the system for the most affluent people. For example, the top of the US medical system is better than European medicine, but it costs a lot and is not available to the huge majority of people. In proportion to GDP, the US health system costs 30 percent more than in Europe, and yet as many as 37 million Americans have no medical insurance at all.

But we also know that the welfare state is not perfect – it tends to be dominated by vested interests, and in many places needs reforms that are hard to implement. But there are progressive ideas in the welfare state, of active involvement and less dependency.

Does an effective welfare state have to be confined to the developed world?

Another positive reason for reforming the welfare state is that across three-quarters of the planet, the welfare state is for the middle class. In the Third World, different policies are needed to provide services, with more self-management where the center provides mainly services such as training. Successful examples include Hong Kong and Singapore. Four decades ago they were still developing countries. Now their private sector is supported by good services but also upgrades labor, and the welfare state has been seen as a development tool. Nothing could be more untrue than the line taken by Milton Friedman and others, who have claimed that the success of Hong Kong was due to the private sector. In fact, the success of Hong Kong and Singapore was something very specific to do with a synergistic relationship between strong government policy (in very subtle ways in Hong Kong), the welfare state, and the competitiveness of the private sector. In other parts of the world the story is also very specific, with different cities in the same country well or badly run.

An example is Brazil, where São Paulo is a badly run city, but Curitiba is a city of two million with good-quality schools and transport. It went from poverty to a real process of development and enhancement of the quality of life, thanks to good local management. Another memorable transformation was Chile in the 1990s. The Pinochet regime managed 1 percent annual growth. In the [post-Pinochet] 1990s growth was much faster, because the welfare state was rebuilt, and the percentage of the population in poverty was halved. The process was open and redistributive at the same time.

Are these things delivered by national governments, or self-managed initiatives?

Both. In Chile the changes were due to government policy. There are fewer successful examples of self-managed reform, but Curitiba is one.

What does this tell us about the future of mixed economies?

A government that can take strong initiatives is essential, but everyone has to understand the role of the welfare state in creating human capital. The economy has to be performance-oriented, and it has to be understood that the economy and the welfare state support each other. The state also needs to operate at an appropriate level. If much of the population is on the edge of ecological catastrophe, as in much of the Third World, the short-term needs are very big. A country in that condition cannot achieve a European welfare state in one leap. It needs both short- and long-term strategies.

And what about the role of the state as ring-holder? In Europe, Japan, or the USA, the police will come if you call, and courts will uphold a contract in court. You have written a lot about the collapse of this sort of trust in Russia after the collapse of the USSR.

Market economies need institutions around them. It has been shown that the US economy was created by the courts and legal judgments. Without such systems you get a "wild economy" and the law of the jungle, as happened in Russia.

I was chair of a committee on this subject in Russia in 1992. We concluded that a new constitution and party system were needed to avoid tanks on the street. We had the right analysis and delivered it to the top people at the right time, and it still did not work. As a result, I always take dealings with politicians with a pinch of salt. These people know what they want to do. [Boris] Yeltsin wanted personal political control more than he wanted reform. Others wanted to be oligarchs, to get rich out of the lawless society. The USA and the IMF essentially accepted high-level Russian corruption. Now, [Vladimir] Putin is trying to impose some level of state control over the oligarchs, while still looking for their help. Putin's support among most Russians results from people's frustration, because they agree with reestablishing state control over mafias and oligarchs. They are still there, but on transformed terms. The power relationship has been reversed, with the state getting more power than under Yeltsin, who was a puppet. This also means that the formal economy is growing, and barter is becoming less dominant.

One result of the changes Putin is making is that Russia has some restored national dignity. It is now a respected power, although not a superpower. After September 11, the Chechens are now regarded internationally as terrorists, not freedom fighters, which they never were. At one point a poll revealed that the majority of Russians thought Nato would attack Russia. Now Russia is a valued US partner against terrorism and a possible Nato member, in an interesting twist of history. . . .

What would you regard as the future for public service in a world where politics and the media overlap so much?

You know I never talk about the future, but I can say that the present systems for financing politics lead to the privatization of the state. Strong, clean, autonomous public servants are the antidote. Japan is one of the most corrupt countries in the world. But it has nationalistic and mostly honest public servants with assured careers who do not need to be bought.

The same applies to British public service. One of our proposals to Yeltsin was to create a Russian version of ENA [the Ecole Nationale d'Administration, the college whose graduates run most of French public life]. I would admit that creating such an elite is democratically dangerous. But in the developed world, political systems are too weak unless such a group exists. Despite Pinochet, such a long-term public service bureaucracy has survived in Chile, and has kept Chile as the cleanest country in Latin America.

There are dangers because such a group tends to be conservative. But on the whole they also believe in preserving the nation. This is usually to the good, although members of such elites can tend to be xenophobic.

Surely in the network world, one of the roles of governments is to be there. A company can move to Mexico to get cheap labor, but the government of Barcelona or Britain has to look after the area whose voters put it in power.

Yes, and this means that they have to find ways to be rooted in national or local space while being active in global networks, especially networks of power and money. One way they do this is to get together with other governments. The EU is the most developed "network state." Its institutions are a typical network, because the European Commission does not have the final power to make decisions. That is the role of national governments. The EU has a complex network geography with many nodes, taking in the European Parliament and many other points, none of which is a center where all decisions are taken. Another part of the system is the European Central Bank, which is independent, but part of the EU machine. Now, national legislation needs European approval, but that means sharing sovereignty, not losing it. The EU network also ties into others, such as the link to Nato for security, and into the rest of the world for aid and international agreements. Likewise, the IMF still has a significant role in international economic policies that affect Europe, and there are significant roles for policy and strategy centers such as the OECD. At its widest, the Bank of Japan and the [US] Federal Reserve are part of the network when it comes to preventing the fall of the euro. And don't forget that these networks operate permanently, not just when emergency action is needed.

Now things are becoming even more interesting, because new nodes are being added. Sub-national levels are becoming more important, as exemplified in the UK by the process of devolution of power initiated by [Prime Minister Tony] Blair. [Power was devolved to Scotland, Wales, Northern Ireland, and London after the 1997 general election, and in 2002 there were plans for English regional assemblies.] Or, the newly developed "state of autonomies" in Spain, giving considerable powers to Catalonia, the Basque country, and other nationalities and regions. The European Committee of Regions represents them and could become the Senate of the European Parliament.

There is also another layer, that of the NGOs, which relate to governments and represent the political privatization of government. They are flexible and act globally, and there are very many of them in the global arena.

The same logic applies in the USA. The network is emerging everywhere as the way for governments to counter their rootedness and enhance their ability to control and negotiate.

If governments are static and money is mobile, do you agree that there is a danger that taxes will become optional for the rich and that state finances will be eroded dangerously?

Ultimately the state is about two things – taxes and violence. This essence does not change much. There is no state without taxes, and that was the weak point of Russia in the 1990s. If corporations won't pay their taxes, the state can't do much – it cannot even build a state accounting system. In Russia, the state under Putin lowered tax rates but made sure corporations paid some.

The key issue is that the mobility of capital and of high-income people reduces the chances of collecting taxes. This is not even illegal. There are firms that simply scan the world looking for tax breaks. And the amount of money involved is enough to have a substantial effect. It is a threat to the stability of governments and is selective. Not everyone can do it. It also opens the door to money laundering.

However, the main problem is the fast turnover of legal money movements, not laundering. The companies and people who do it inject chaos into the system. Rich people always think they know better than governments what to do with their money. This means that the global regulation of financial flows has to start with closing tax havens. There is no chance that this will happen in the short term, but maybe a global financial crash – which I think is unlikely – would cause it to become a priority. After all, the present moves to close tax havens only gained momentum after September 11, when it became apparent that [the militant Muslim organization] al-Qaeda was using them for money transmission. At that point, initiatives that could have happened years before suddenly started. The same applies to hedge funds. The collapse of LTCM [Long-Term Capital Management] was the cue for them to be overseen more intensely, because of the damage to people's assets that such crashes cause. The markets bounced back quickly, but the assets and people immediately affected are slow to recover.

Mention of tax havens and financial regulation brings us to something that emerges in The Information Age *as a key concern of yours – crime, especially large-scale international crime. You see it as a full participant in the network economy, although your writing leaves no doubt that you regard it as an evil.*

Crime is a very important and growing part of the world economy. In some ways it is not different from the other key elements of that economy. It uses similar networks, it diversifies in similar ways, it has a similar division of labor, and it understands markets in the same way. And it operates on a large and increasing scale. I regard it as an unwelcome vote of confidence that Latin American criminals read my work. But one reason is that this area is one of the greatest failures of most contemporary social science. It has failed to acknowledge the new importance of the criminal economy.

There are some people and organizations that have some awareness of the issue. For example, I spoke at a conference when [Fernando] Cardoso took over as president of Brazil, and I emphasized the importance of the criminal economy in the world. The economists agreed – but said that they must ignore crime as a relevant factor because there is no way to gather good data on it. I think that although it is a big and risky challenge, there is no choice but to do serious work on it. You cannot leave it to journalists. The only part that is really dangerous is when you want to name the person doing something illegal, but for a social scientist that is not vital. If you leave that out, it is possible to do all sorts of research.

How central are drugs to the international criminal economy?

They are vital: they make up about 60 percent of its total business. But there are many other aspects. One is the trade in people. Chinese criminals use profits from immigration crimes to fund other types of crime. Also important are weapons, including, perhaps, weapons of mass destruction. But drugs vary in their illegality. One way to fight the drug traffic is to legalize it. Like smoking, if it is legal, you can then think about how it might be treated. In the USA and elsewhere in the developed world, the percentage of the population that smokes has come down hugely, and the habit will become largely eradicated. Likewise, public health measures could cut drug use massively if there were not such a massive attempt to repress it. In the USA, 45 percent of people in jail are there because of drugs in some way, either trafficking in them or using them. There is life imprisonment for three counts of drug use, let alone trafficking. Traffickers hate drug legalization, but they know they have little to fear, because politicians cannot be seen to condone drugs.

What about the interaction between this trade and conventional power systems?

The most destructive effect is on institutions, not people. Colombia is the best-known case. It cannot solve its political problems without dealing with the criminal economy. But there are direct links to the [2002] economic and political crisis in Argentina. And in Mexico the drug cartels have penetrated the state completely. Elsewhere in the world, the political influence of the Japanese Yakuza is well known. In each case, criminals are business leaders who need, and have, close connections with other business leaders, politicians, and the rest. This corrupts the whole system. Likewise, the effects of drugs have completely altered the US justice system. When a 15-year-old sells drugs in a school in the USA, he or she is the local manifestation of a global crime system – in other words, a node in a fully developed network.

Of course, drugs are only part of the story. In the network it is possible to trade almost anything illegal. Art, endangered species, people. But drug legalization would weaken the system a lot, as the US gangs of the 1930s were weakened by the end of Prohibition [the temporary ban on alcoholic drink].

Are justice systems also affected by the growth of the network world?

Yes, the fight against global crime is bound to alter the way justice works. Baltasar Garzon, the Spanish judge who attempted to get [former Chilean dictator Augusto] Pinochet tried in Spain for crimes committed against Spaniards in Chile, was a case in point. He used the Spanish link to attempt to prosecute someone who was not in Spain. If justice becomes nonterritorial, this would be a fundamental revolution. In Belgium it is possible to prosecute for crimes not committed in Belgium. The USA has now started to take an interest in this, and is debating a redefinition of this aspect of the role of the state, although until now the US government has refused to accept the jurisdiction of an International Court over its citizens. If the process of globalization of justice continues, it might involve a world court or perhaps world proceedings in a national court. In Europe there is interest in a common arrest warrant, which would allow people accused of particular crimes to be repatriated by any European police force. The Spanish are especially keen, because they would love to get their hands on Basque terrorists in France. But on a bigger scale there could be cross-border police action, as well as prosecution, to match the growth of global crime.

World policing is a new development. Everyone knows about Interpol, but that is more of a data exchange machine than a police force. But it is likely that all police forces in Europe will become internationalized, which is interesting, because it shows the network state we mentioned above in action in one of the most traditional areas of the public sector. And the same will come to apply to courts as well as the police.

Will the same dynamic bring in other countries as well?

The USA is the slowest major nation to get involved in these developments and in most other international initiatives. It is likely to be the world's last nation-state. But it is not clear that the rest of the world will want to accept this. At some point even the USA will realize that it is in a global network world and join in the systems that make it up.

For the moment, the USA has not got over the end of the cold war in terms of its own behavior. But I think this is likely to change, and the biggest factor will be the way in which US firms are rooted all over the world. They must realize that no one state can manage the world economy or deal with the highly intertwined global problems that shape our lives.

Conversation 7

Castells's World Tour

MARTIN INCE *Your working life, especially the writing of The
Information Age, has involved massive world travel and, more
importantly, hard fieldwork and research in many countries.
Countries, cities, and regions appear in abundance throughout
this book, but here we are going to get your opinion about the
issues and problems of the areas we do not cover, and revisit the
ones mentioned elsewhere in a more systematic way. Naturally
your aversion to forecasting and prediction will be respected, but
feel free to be opinionated in an evidence-based way.*

*You said when we met in Barcelona that the only part of the
world you have not physically visited is the Middle East (we did
not mention Antarctica). So I'll ask you about it.*

*We are having this conversation early in 2002. We agreed last
year that the attacks on the USA of 11 September 2001 do not
raise any fundamental new issues. Indeed, you point to the part
of* The Information Age *(page 387 of the second edition) in
which attacks such as those of 11 September 2001 are raised as
a possibility. At the same time, near-warfare between Israel and
its neighbors is killing more people than ever, and is defying
local and world efforts to find a solution.*

MANUEL CASTELLS Well, I really do not know the region
myself, but I have had so many good Arab and Muslim students (particularly Palestinians and Saudis), and know so
many people from the Arab culture that I think I know the
basic data, and have a deep sensitivity to the issue. I must
say, I am a strong defender of the existence of Israel, but also

have a very deep critique of Israeli expansionism, and of the systemic oppression they have practiced against the Palestinians. [Ariel] Sharon does represent a very deep current in Israel, obviously fed by history. I do not think Israel can truly accept the existence of an independent Palestinian state without active pressure from the international community, including the United States. Of course, [Palestinian leader Yasser] Arafat and company are partly responsible for this (remember the early calls to throw all Jews into the sea), but, objectively speaking, Israel is the oppressor, and its existence is imperilled only by itself, by making the entire Palestinian population into human time bombs. Israel does have enough protection from the outside world, and from its own nuclear weapons. It just needs to settle for peace, forgetting about the Great Israel, and the additional one million Jews, and engaging in peaceful cooperation with its Arabian neighbors and its own Arab citizens.

Next an old question that still needs answering. Is the vast wealth of the Middle East, developed from oil and concentrated very narrowly, necessarily going to be used in confrontations with a developed world which seems happy to take its product while ignoring its values?

Well, things are not so simple. Oil is by and large controlled by the West, either directly or through arrangements with the Saudis and the Emirates, and the West never cares too much about the religious fundamentalism of the Saudis, and in fact encouraged it as a vaccine against communism and radical nationalism. Iran and Iraq are different; but, frankly, Iran is essentially connected to other oil consumers, such as Japan and China, besides Western Europe. Furthermore, it is a well-known fact that the USA supported the origins of al-Qaeda in Afghanistan, against the Soviets, and that in 1996 the Taliban came to power with the support of Pakistan and Saudi Arabia, and the consent of the USA, which saw them as a more stable force. So let us say that fundamentalism, or even fanaticism, has never bothered the US government in its realpolitik, and women in Afghanistan could be oppressed by the Taliban without much interference from the Clinton administration. It is when the defense of Islamic identity threatened by the Westernization of Saudi Arabia, and by the unrelenting support of the USA for Israeli expansionism, alienates some of the dissident elites of the Arab world that the USA realizes the threat. The issue, then, is how to react against the radical fundamentalists while keeping the alliance with the moderate fundamentalists who are at the same time the guardians of the holy sites and the guardians of Western oil. This is why the thesis of the clash of civilizations is a primitive ethnocentric ideology that does not acknowledge the complexity of the interplay between identity, geopolitics, and economic interests. The longer ago the colonial past, the thinner the penetration and the understanding of the Arab and Muslim cultures, precisely because the Arab and Muslim leaders close to the West are Westernized, and we think we know their countries because we know them well. But they have a split personality, and a split culture, because the moment they become fully Westerners, they cease to be part of the Muslim world, thus losing the source of their wealth, influence, and power. So there is, and will be, a tension between the Westernization of the Muslim world (meaning global capitalism and political democracy) and the integration of the Muslims in a shared world. The agents of democracy (the Muslim leaders) cannot really accept democracy (they would be ousted in all likelihood) or some fundamental social change, such as the end of patriarchalism.

When the USA looks at the Middle East, it does so in a way that seems odd to Europeans. Despite the many Muslims who live in the USA, there seems to be little knowledge of their concerns or culture (although I may be misled by the contrast with the UK, because I live in Muslim Britain). Do your conversations lead you to think that the USA may now take a more informed approach to the Muslim world? Or is it more likely that the prompt collapse of the Taliban under US attack will lead the US authorities to decide that firepower is more use than knowledge?

Radical fundamentalism has not collapsed, not even in
Afghanistan. This is not a great military victory. The roots of
fundamentalism are alive and well, and thus the war, this
strange netwar, will go on for a long time. In this the US
government is right, and therefore military action, led by
technology, is taking precedence over understanding. The
unilateral US policy towards Israel, with no real opening for
the Palestinians, in spite of the Saudi efforts to offer peace,
is a clear example of the difficulty. It is not only to protect
Israel, it is using the formidable Israeli shield to protect the
USA. No, I do not think that the USA either understands the
Muslim world or cares to do so. And you can see a growing
anti-Muslim feeling among the American people.

*There has, I think, always been a specific reason for the low
level of US engagement with the Muslim world, which is the
strength of the Israeli lobby in US politics. The importance of
Israel to politicians wanting to be elected has contrasted with
the vital need for Middle Eastern oil. The upshot has been the
privatization of a large area of US foreign policy – presidents
talking to Israel while oil companies talk to Saudi Arabia. Is
there a realization now that this has meant ignorance and
disengagement that has had a high price?*

No, the Israeli connection will be deeper and deeper. Not
only because of the power of the lobby in the US election,
but because Israel is the bedrock of American geopolitics and
military power in a decisive area of the world. In this sense,
there is no contradiction between Jewish influence in the
USA and the US national security interest. It would be different if the USA would engage in the building of a more
stable world on the basis of shared development, multicultural dialogue, and multilateral institutionalization of global
governance. But these are empty words in the foreseeable US
foreign policy.

*The Middle East has also been the focus of the two most recent
world attacks on perceived international evildoers – the 2001/2*

war in Afghanistan and the Gulf War a decade earlier. Both are regarded as more successful than interventions in Somalia or the former Yugoslavia. Is there a danger that the area will become a free-fire zone for US intervention, as Latin America was a generation earlier?

There is a danger of US military intervention (bombing and special operations) around the world, in any area from where it could be thought terrorist attacks could be staged against US interests. There is a process of globalization of a new form of war, the netwar, in the terminology of the experts of the Rand Corporation.

Equally, an event such as the September 11 attacks does require a response. Its initial cause was dissatisfaction with the Westernization of Saudi Arabia – which to external observers might not seem to have gone very far yet. Making Saudi Arabia a more democratic state might be agreeable to liberals like us, but how do we cope with the fact that it would be a change for the worse for many Muslims?

Of course, the irony is that the Saudis are not the excluded of the Muslim world, so this is clearly a matter of religious identity being marginalized in the view of traditionalists. The real issue is if this identity politics would connect with the reaction of the socially excluded throughout the Muslim world, as in Pakistan. This is Bin Laden's bet. If this succeeds, there is no technology that can stop hundreds of millions of fanatical, impoverished people who could react both in terms of their religious faith and in terms of their insurgency against social exclusion. This is why the policy of shared development on a gigantic scale is the only way to deactivate this time bomb. Al-Qaeda is not dangerous in itself, as Lenin was not a threat to capitalism until Russia collapsed, but if the poor Muslim countries look for saviors in the privileged classes of Muslim clerics, fueled by a portion of the oil wealth, then we have the equation that haunts the US establishment. The difficulty is that, rather than treating the problem, they believe they can just do radical surgery through military technology.

As a British taxpayer, I regard getting rid of the Taliban as one of the better things the state has spent my money on in recent years. But the Taliban only became the enemy because of its role in housing al-Qaeda. Many politicians have spoken of the need to make Afghanistan a better place, if only to prevent its becoming once again a haven for evildoers. Do the examples of multinational intervention elsewhere in the world give you hope of success here or fill you with foreboding?

No. I think your money, and mine, has been misspent. We could have captured Bin Laden in Tora Bora, and we missed him because we used millions of dollars in bombing to avoid risking American and British troops on the ground. And we probably underpaid our Afghan warlords, who most likely took more money from the other side to let him go. Most multinational interventions fail because they lack clear objectives, and have no real policy behind them. It is always a band-aid to wait and see, because there is no strategy for dealing with the real problems of societies: development, sharing the wealth, and sharing the power through institution building. It is just to stop the carnage and go as soon as our security problems are settled. As Bush said, no nation building. But no nation building means that the nations build themselves, on their own grounds – usually against so-called Western interests.

Is it possible that the picture will change radically in coming years because the oil century – the twentieth – has been and gone? Might that mean that the Middle East will lose its significance if this is the century of solar power, wind farms, and energy efficiency? Would that mean more desperation, and drive fundamentalism?

Unfortunately, oil is here to stay for a long time, but yes, the more the region were impoverished, the more the explosive connection between identity and exclusion would accelerate – look at Egypt.

What is the argument between Israel and its neighbors about? Are there borders or systems that can solve it, or is an armed truce the best we can hope for? Might better systems and politicians in Palestine and Israel help? Can a cycle of violence like that really be broken by conflict resolution methods? Or (like Ireland) does change have to come about because of forces in the outside world – for example, in this case in the USA?

To start with, these are two fundamentalisms. The way Israelis feel about Jerusalem can only be understood in terms of identity politics, and there is a symmetrical reaction from the Arabs. Both forget that Jerusalem is also a Christian holy site. But then, there is the colonial foundation of Israel out of the justified guilt feelings of the world, and particularly of Europeans, because of the Holocaust – and the endless persecutions of Jews throughout our history. Then there is the utilization of the Palestinians by undemocratic Arab states to feed their nationalism and their ambitions. Then there is the inflammatory rhetoric of the Palestinian leadership over a long time, and the bloody terrorist attacks, answered in kind by the Israelis. And then there is the constant humiliation of the Arab world by Israel, a Western outpost in military, technological, and economic terms. And then there is Israeli expansionism, with hundreds of thousands of Jews coming from oppressed, poor lands in the Arab world and in the ex-Soviet Union. On the other hand, there are generation after generation of Palestinian children growing up in hatred, but also being rather well educated and employed by the Israelis, in appalling conditions, so there is also a class struggle involved there, together with identity and nationalism and democracy. All this is too much to be solved by rational negotiation. The world must understand that a solution must be imposed – and I mean imposed – from the outside on both sides, to create material conditions for both Jews and Palestinians to realize that another life is possible. If the international community does not proceed along these lines, the Middle East will continue to destabilize the whole world, making the progress of humankind impossible because of the multiple sources of this conflict. It is the oldest and most intractable conflict that is anchoring us in the most primitive form of existence, around intolerance and violence. Either we confront this, or we will be engulfed by the deterioration of the conflict. But I am utterly pessimistic about our capacity to intervene, because the USA will just say no.

Let's alight briefly in the other major countries of the region. Iraq: are all bets off while Saddam stays in power? Would you agree that a functioning civil society can be developed there after he goes more readily than in, say, Afghanistan? Might Iraq provide a precedent for dictators being pushed out of power because of their actions against their own people rather than outside their borders?

If the USA has not launched an all-out war against Iraq, it is simply because it is not sure what to do afterwards. Saddam is a bloody dictator, and a dangerous man – he would build nuclear weapons or biological weapons capability if he could do it. The problem is that he has effectively subdued his society, and any attempts to impose something else from outside, by using bombs, would most likely meet with the hostility of the Iraqi people. It is not certain, because Milosevic was ousted at the same time by Nato bombs and by Serb democrats, but I am afraid Iraq has a much less developed civil society and political opposition, and nationalism against the West is still paramount. Besides, the West always supported Iraq to counter Iran – until it went out of control, as often happens. So, I think matters will muddle through, until the USA or Israel decides it's time to act against Iraq before it gets too dangerous, paying the price of a full-fledged war and subsequent military occupation (probably by British troops, who specialize in the cleaning-up stage after the mess).

Post-thought added in September 2002

In September 2002 it appears clear that fear and narrow domestic political interest have convinced the Bush administration to go to war with Iraq, until Saddam would be deposed and a puppet regime (Afghan-style) could be established. In their view, this would remove a potential support for terrorist groups, a source of concern regarding the possession of weapons of mass destruction by an unreliable country, and, not least, direct Western control of the second largest oil reserves in the world. In addition, having Iraqi oil under control will facilitate a tougher attitude to the Saudis, whose involvement in financing al-Qaeda has now been exposed.

However, this war, about to break out when we speak, may trigger very serious, unpredictable chain reactions, and could also reactivate the war in Afghanistan, extend the conflict to Kashmir, destabilize Pakistan, and engulf much of the world in violence and destruction. The USA simply does not know what it is starting, because, fundamentally, it has decided on fully-fledged unilateralism, building its security exclusively on its military strength. This is extremely dangerous, for the United States as well as for the Arab countries, for Israel, and for the world at large.

Iran: is it really a sponsor of international terror, or is it more a society struggling with reform?

It is at the same time a fundamentalist state and a modern state trying to open the way for a very active, evolved, and democratic society. You know that my trilogy has been published in Iran without censorship? Either I am a fundamentalist, or Iran is becoming a very diverse intellectual culture – there is evidence that it is the latter.

Turkey: is it an EU candidate country with a secular society and Western ambitions? Or is it Asia Minor, a Middle Eastern country fighting its own people in Kurdistan and suppressing them throughout the rest of its territory?

Turkey is a fully European society. It they were not Muslims, there would not even be a doubt about this for anybody. The Kurds are certainly oppressed, but other nationalities in

Europe were oppressed by dictatorships (for example, Basques and Catalans in Spain under Franco), and this did not disqualify Spain as European – although it was not a democracy. So the real issue in Turkey is the insufficient development of democratic institutions and respect for human rights. It was convenient to Nato to strengthen the Turkish army in the southern flank of the Soviet Union, and now Turkish society has to digest its own army in stages. The recipe is development and democracy. And for this, joining the EU is essential. Would the EU dare to acknowledge that we do not like Muslim countries in the Union? Maybe we could agree with Berlusconi and make Christianity an essential component of European identity. I think this is an ethnocentric, untenable, and dangerous proposition. In fact, in the book I have just co-edited entitled *Muslim Europe* (2002), we show the growing multiculturalism of Europe. Muslims are now, and will be, an inextricable part of European societies.

Next, Asia: with most of the world's people, some of its most intractable problems, and much of its greatest potential. Many of the most substantial issues we need to discuss come under headings that I would characterize as the collapse of the Soviet Union, the aftermath of the Japanese bubble, the future of the Tiger economies, and, as separate items, the prospects for China and India. The cold war casts a long shadow. What will the establishment of a functioning civil society in Russia mean for the Far East?

As you know, I do not make predictions. Instead, one comment. People tend to forget that Russia is an Asian Pacific country, and that the longest Russian border is with China. Furthermore, Siberia is perhaps the area in the world with the largest reserves of strategic natural resources, including fuels, hydroelectric energy, rare metals, forestry products, and the like. These are exactly the resources that Japan, Korea, and China lack dearly. So major economic growth in these countries, particularly in China, leads to dependence on the supply of these natural resources, which gives the opportunity for complementarity between Siberia and the Russian Far East and the Asian Pacific. As Emma Kiselyova and I entitled our study of the matter, Siberia is the missing link in the Asian Pacific Development scheme.

The last place on Earth with a cold war and an iron curtain is Korea. Are they sustainable?

People do not understand the depth of Korean national identity. Both Koreas want and need reunification. The problem is the vested interests of both sides, and the ideologies that disguise these interests. If the South Korean oligarchs offer a real chance to the North Korean Communist leaders to become part of the national oligarchy, the country will be reunified, to the great joy of the whole Korean people.

The North Korean nuclear threat is a bogey man of the US hawks. I would say that the only real remnants of the cold war are in the minds of some unreconstructed members of the American foreign policy establishment.

Japan: its prime position in the postwar world has been as a US ally, not a defeated opponent, freed by disarmament to put resources into economic development and producing the world's longest-lived population. Japan's social system was well suited to the era of mass production, but it has become far less dynamic in the more informal network age. Can it work out a way to succeed in an era where merit counts for more than status?

Again, no predictions. But I have analyzed, in volume 3 of my trilogy, the contradiction between the Japanese cultural, political, and industrial structure and the flexibility and innovation required in the network society and in the network economy. It is ironic, because Japan (meaning MITI, the former Ministry of International Trade and Industry) invented the notion of the Information Society (*Johoka Sakai* in Japanese) in 1969, and the French experts Alain Minc and Pierre Nora imported it into the West in 1978. But the Japanese version was made out of robots and futurology, machines and consumer goods, with very little about cultural transformation since, of course, the Japanese culture must not be changed in their view. In other words, the future was painted as a super-industrial society, preserving and enhancing the natural order of the state and global corporations, with subdued people made happy through consumption. Then there was a shift to deregulation, true globalization (not just one-sided trade between Japan and the world), media penetration of Japanese culture, the strategic importance of software over hardware, the Internet and horizontal rather than top-down communication, and individual innovation and entepreneurial risk taking as the sources of wealth and power. On top of this, an absolutely corrupt, and inefficient, political system and a well-meaning bureaucracy that was unable to understand the world in transformation because they believed their own experts, selected by their acceptance of the basic postulates of the bureaucracy.

The result of this failure to adapt to the network society and to the new economy was permanent economic stagnation, a loss of political legitimacy, and cultural insecurity, as the generational divide blocked communication between parents and children, undermining the principle of authority upon which the Japanese society is made. And women started to revolt, bringing down another pillar of Japan's national specificity. Overall, the all-mighty Japan became one of the least performing countries in the world. By the way, this shows how unfounded were the fears of all those social scientists and management experts in the USA who made their business in the 1980s by stirring the fear of Japan as number one, which could threaten US hegemony. International trade was not, and is not, the main dimension of globalization, and Japan's technological ability to copy US innovation and produce it more cheaply was an easy trick, whose advantage vanished as soon as Japan reached the frontier of innovation. Beyond this frontier, the Japanese education system was unable to move forward, because it is designed to pass exams up the ladder, and to learn how to execute instructions, just the contrary of what is needed in an innovation-driven economy, based on entrepreneurialism.

Neither the Japanese state nor its American critics understood the deep crisis of Japan, rooted in its institutional (not cultural, not by any means) incapacity to adapt to the information age, an age made of networks and multiculturalism.

Would Japan's new combined ministry of education and research be well advised to end attempts to mold the national character?

Any attempt to mold the national character is, in fact, an expression of the affirmation of a national character. The issue is to free society, to free people who are exposed to global media and to the Internet, to make up their own lives, and in doing so, they will change for ever a society based on status, authoritarian hierarchies, nationalism, and, to a large extent, fear of the outside world.

Will Japan be able to overcome racism to welcome foreign people and ideas? How fatal would it be to stick to its previous cultural uniformity?

Nothing is fatal in life. I doubt that Japan can continue to be uniform in a world of flows of images, sounds, information, and immigrants. The issue is not if Japan can remain the same in the midst of a globalized world – it cannot. The issue is the cost, and the internal convulsions through which this process of adaptation and change will take place.

The Tiger economies. The success of Hong Kong, Singapore, South Korea, and Taiwan has been analyzed widely and involved a unique mix of state enterprise and an ambitious private sector, with few allowances for democratic preferences. These societies have also been very open to external influences. Do they have systems in place to cope with lower growth and more public expectations – for example, in terms of environmental protection?

The tigers diverged sharply in their historical trajectories once they became fully developed economies. Taiwan and

South Korea have now vibrant civil societies, and quite con-
flictive democracies. Also, they have shown a great deal of
initiative in shifting gear to the Information Age and to the
new, global economy. South Korea is the most advanced
country in the world in terms of diffusion of broadband
Internet (half the population), and the chaebol [large cor-
porations] have been restructured and somewhat curtailed in
their power. Taiwan has become a lifeline for Silicon Valley,
and is engaged at the frontier of high-tech manufacturing,
fully integrated into the global networks of electronics. In
addition, Taiwanese capitalism is fully deployed in southern
China. You cannot understand China's development today
without the Taiwan connection, as documented by Berkeley
professor You-tien Hsing. Hong Kong has become one of the
three leading financial and advanced centers of China (the
others, of course, are Shanghai and Beijing) and the main
connecting point between China and the global economy,
and could very soon be one of the major nodes. And Hong
Kong is building local networks to form the largest metropolitan region in the world, Hong Kong–Shenzhen–Canton–
Pearl River Delta–Zhuhai–Macau, with about 50 million
people working in this interconnected area, an economic
powerhouse, and a major metropolitan experiment.

As for Singapore, this continues to be the only successful
Leninist experience in history, a one-party-led development
model, a highly authoritarian system, but insuring development and good living conditions to its population in
exchange for submission of their liberty. It is also the only
example of a fruitful connection between foreign multina-
tionals and a developmental state. The issue is how long
Singapore can keep an authoritarian state and culture in the
context of an increasingly assertive civil society. Besides,
Singapore is the Israel of Southeast Asia (and actually its
armed forces are trained and equipped by Israel), so rising
ethnic and religious tensions in the region may jeopardize its
safety, with unpredictable consequences. Singapore would
certainly like to link up with China and become a point of
technology transfer, but the issue is how much the Chinese

are ready to pay the price of potential hostility from the larger Southeast Asian environment.

China: what happens once the current generation of its rulers dies out? Is the state capitalist model they secured likely to be stable?

The problem in China is not the new generation, but the older one. There is a Western myth that the problem of China is political democracy. This has never existed in China, and at the time democracy is being de-legitimized in the world, it is unlikely to inspire the Chinese masses to take up the risk, particularly if access to consumer goods and contact with the West continues. The real problem is for the large sectors of the population living off unproductive industries and obsolete public bureaucracies that are being closed down. If the process of attrition is not fast enough, these dis-affected masses are prone to revolt against a regime that has abandoned them, and they are already turning to messianic movements, such as Falun Gong, claiming to defend Chinese traditions against destructive foreign influence and corrupt rulers. This is why the Chinese Communists fear Falun Gong more than anything else.

Is there the prospect of a Soviet-type economic revolution replacing the state and military with more conventional capitalists?

Absolutely not. The alternatives are between a 1970s Brazil-like capitalist economy, with powerful segments, and a large middle class, connected to the global economy, under the protection of a nondemocratic state, and, on the other hand, a messianic, poor people's revolt, based on identity and com-munalism, that would create a new wave of internal wars, with extraordinary disruptive potential for the world at large.

Is there a bloodless way to get there?

To the globalized, capitalist China, yes, by buying enough people through development, and repressing selectively enough to avoid a massive backlash. All will depend on media control, and on isolating the domestic economy from the shocks of financial global markets – to keep the renmin bi [the Chinese currency] not convertible, and to win the ideological battle against the religious traditionalists, via TV and the Internet.

India: do you believe that it is "the world's largest democracy"?

It is. But it is also the country with the largest number of poor people in the world, and a country where castes still rule, and where Hindu and Muslim fundamentalism are the driving forces in society. It is a country of extraordinary contradictions that is fueling an increasingly aggressive brand of nationalism. At the same time, the educated class of India is one of the most educated groups in the world, with an extraordinary blend of Western and Eastern culture, science, and philosophy. India is also a great reservoir of technological minds, probably the best engineers in the world. But the relationship between the poor and the state is unsettled, as shown in the great book by Indian professor Ananya Roy.

Is it going to split economically between a high-technology state and a huge expanse of the Fourth World?

This is already an empirical observation.

Will such a split exacerbate the pressures that (as we write) are causing renewed race- and religion-based bloodshed?

Undoubtedly. Identity cannot be reduced to economic conditions and to poverty, but what happens is that identity-based politics gives control of government that is key to distributing resources, particularly for the poor. So, class struggle, political patronage, and identity politics make a very dangerous mixture.

Finally in Asia, Australia, and New Zealand: can their "England in the Sun" model succeed in the network age without their becoming much more honest about their Asian status and shaping policies accordingly?

Australia and New Zealand are not the same. New Zealand is much more interesting, because it is one of the most socially progressive countries in the world. But they both have the same problem: how to be part of the Asian Pacific (their great economic opportunity) without being culturally overwhelmed – which would provoke an ethnic nationalist backlash. I guess that they may end up adopting the Singapore model of high-level islands in the globality, rather than reinventing England – a country that was not so kind to their ancestors. Probably Australian soap operas and New Zealand eco-tourism are their industries of the future. Oooops! The future!

Next stop, America. Can a country where the work of Charles Darwin is regarded as controversial be taken seriously?

Much more seriously than a fully secularized Europe. Religion is a fundamental dimension of human existence, as it is spirituality in the broadest sense. And religious identity is increasing all over the world as a source of meaning. It is only Europe that feels that it is beyond this need.

This would mean the absolute triumph of reason, but we know this is not the case; we know that people have some deeper feelings, about love, about search, about fear, about protection, that cannot be found in their immediate experience. I believe that the fact that in Europe religion became institutionalized in oppressive apparatuses very early in the historical experience at the same time insured the durability of Christianity but also cut it off from the inner life of many people. America, and the rest of the world, has a more personal, flexible approach to religion, sometimes as a deep experience, but sometimes also as a consumer good or as soap opera, which makes religion more human and, ultimately, more effective in securing people in a world of fear and aggression. So, America is a very religious country, but so is the large majority of the world.

*Today [March 2002] the United States' international competi-
tors are rejoicing at legislation that will mean its abandoning
wide areas of cloning research. For them it is a business opportunity. But does it show that, despite the immense power of
corporate America, politicians there have to be aware of a much
more complex balance of power, including many identity
groups which reject discoveries that might be regarded as con-
tradicting Holy Writ, or Papal teaching?*

Well, the record shows that while American identity includes
religion as a key feature, research in American universities
surpasses in quality, quantity, and daring experimentation
research in Europe or anywhere else in the world, mainly
through researchers from other countries who must go to
the USA to be able to innovate. So, flexible institutions and
entrepreneurialism largely offset the obscurantism of some
dogmas and the opportunism of some politicians. Cloning
will be opposed also in Europe, on other grounds, particularly because public opinion is against it. And in the USA,
unlike in Europe, government-financed research is much less
important than research financed by firms, private founda-
tions, and universities themselves. So, no. No competitive
edge for Europe because of religious conservatism in
America.

*Does the sheer size of the USA mean that it can be the world's
leading generator of new ideas and businesses and at the same
time house millions of people who like the gadgets the modern
age produces (cars, cell phones, satellite TV) but have no respect
for the insights of the twentieth and twenty-first centuries?*

This depends on what you mean by these insights. It is true
that humanities, and academic research, are less connected
to society in the USA than in Europe. America is, by and
large, a much less educated society than Europe, mainly
because of the bad quality of the public school system in
most of the USA. But at the same time, research and innovation in humanities and the arts in the USA is as good as in
Europe, and in many fields, superior. Here, again, many artists

and writers (including writers in other languages than English), and moviemakers, and musicians, and designers, live and work in the USA because it is where the milieu of innovation tends to be, where there is a density of creation and a cosmopolitan attitude towards culture. Thus, the USA is, at the same time, a not very educated society and the depository of much of humankind's creative potential.

Is the pluralism that made Harvard and Berkeley, Apple and Microsoft, also the key to the existence of right-wing militias, enthusiastic support for firearms and capital punishment, and all the other aspects of the USA that make it such a foreign country for Europeans?

Yes, the USA is an extremely specific culture and society, because it is a frontier creation, and always continues to be so. It is an immigrant society, a society made up of people who had to leave their countries to be able to do what they wanted, and distrusted government to do more than what is necessary, because they usually escaped from their own governments back home. In New York City in 2002, over half of the population is foreign-born, and the proportion of WASPs (White Anglo-Saxon Protestants) is less than 10 percent. California is already one-third Latino, and will be over 50 percent in 2030, with the so-called White population (already under 50 percent) amounting by then to about one-third of all Californians. This multiethnicity and immigrant character is at the root of many of the specific cultural features of America.

Insofar as Europe opens up to immigration and becomes multiethnic, it may become closer to some parts of American culture. But overall, America has been produced from the rest of the world, by rejecting the institutions of the former countries while keeping the cultures they come from, and finding forms of cultural reconstruction in the new context. This is an absolutely unique experience, although Argentina, Canada, and Australia could have been similar. They are not, because American capitalism changed the dimensions of the phenomenon, becoming a permanent magnet for the rest of the world.

The economic story of the postwar USA was a successful one despite these internal pressures and fierce international competition, largely overcome despite panics about Japan and other rivals. In the political sphere, the USA is the partner that everyone wants, as we see from Palestine to Ireland. And although defeat in Vietnam has left deep scars, there is no rival to US armed might. Why does this not give Americans and their society a higher comfort factor with the outside world than they seem to have?

Well, the twin towers and Pentagon attack means they are vulnerable, in fact more than ever in their history – save the threat of a planetary nuclear holocaust during the cold war. You see, the notion of the American superpower is a myth, as Joseph Nye has argued with different words. True, there is no match for American military power. But this does not make it possible for America to bomb all the important countries or areas: Europe, Russia, China, Japan, India, Pakistan, and the like. So, yes, it is possible to bomb Afghanistan or Iraq or, eventually, Colombia. But this does not add substantial power. The real threats for America in security terms, as the security establishment rightly acknowledges, are the global terrorist networks. And these are fought with information, not just bombs, and, later on, with the ability to undermine the nurturing ground for terrorism in terms of living conditions and cultural/religious identity.

Even the so-called success of the Afghan war has to be questioned. At this point, in spring 2002, Bin Laden and Mullah Omar have not been captured, and a few hundred Talibs and al-Qaeda members can be easily replaced. The financial and logistical infrastructure of al-Qaeda is not destroyed, and the possibilities for devastating attacks are still there. In other words, the USA is a superpower of the industrial age that is only now starting to build up defenses against the netwars of the information age. For these netwars, the USA cannot proceed with its current unilateralism. It needs cooperation, information, cultural and political ability to penetrate the networks. And, more fundamentally, it needs to engage in a shared development strategy to build a more stable world.

The real American superiority is its university system (the source of science and technology), its openness to the world, and thus to valuable immigration, its institutional flexibility, its entrepreneurial culture, and its ability through the media to propel its way of life throughout the whole world. The ideology of freedom, epitomized in the American way of life, appeals to the young, to the independently minded, and to the daring in all countries [see conversation 2].

I am not going to try to get you to predict whether the USA can overcome the contradictions of its many identities, cultures, and societies. But do you think that the USA has too much momentum to be displaced as the world's leading economy?

To rank economies by country is an old way of thinking. The global economy is made up of networks of companies, not of nations. However, the most dynamic and valuable nodes of these networks are disproportionately in the USA, because of the size of its market, its capacity for innovation, its dynamic labor market, and the efficiency of its capital markets. This is unlikely to change, because of institutional rigidities in the other economies. On the other hand, America has staggering social problems and lags in education in general, a problem that is only compensated for through immigration. So, the security concerns, closing the borders somewhat, may jeopardize the strategy of human resources at the source of productivity.

And as its leading source of innovation and cultural products?

Innovation is a function of the university system and of institutional flexibility; so, on both counts, the US environment has a decisive advantage. Cultural products could change, particularly if the Internet plays a major role in distributing

content from everywhere, and if creators from other countries find connections to satellite TV and global multimedia
networks.

*What are the dangers to this dominant position? An education
system that is too variable in quality? The let's-all-sue-each-
other culture? The costs of providing basic public services at
private expense?*

It is mainly the lack of a modern welfare state. The welfare
state is the basis of productivity in the knowledge economy,
and also the foundation for social stability – a decisive feature
in a complex and violent world. Also, the obsession with
national security could jeopardize liberty, and without liberty
there is no innovation. Besides, as I said, the priority for security will restrict immigration, and immigration is essential to
the American model.

*Or the fact that the vast wealth the USA has generated has been
shared very narrowly?*

Inequality is not so important for people, if they all (or most)
improve. Thirteen percent of people in poverty (and 18
percent of children) is a moral scandal, but does not affect
the other 87 percent of the population too much. Polariza-
tion would be more important, meaning a declining standard
for the lower middle class, but this has been corrected in the
last few years thanks to the new economy.

*And just how seriously do you take the anti-globalization move-
ment, which is mainly opposed to US companies and symbols?*

Very seriously, particularly the current alternative globalization movement (for example, Porto Alegre, the Brazil conference set up as the rival to the Davos meeting of global
capitalism) that accepts globalization as a reality but aims at
changing the world. This is the most important movement
nowadays, and it is changing the terms of the debate through
its influence on public opinion all over the world.

Are anti-globalizers in fact frequent fliers who choose to oppose some US influence around the world while expanding it in other areas?

No, anti-globalizers are people organized around the Internet who refuse structural changes that affect their lives without allowing them to participate in the decisions underlying these changes.

It is impossible to discuss Latin America without reference to US politics. Can the two be decoupled?

Unfortunately, no. Latin America continues to be heavily influenced by what happens in the USA and around US interests. The civil war in Colombia may become very dangerous for the region, and the USA supported the attempted *coup* against [President Hugo] Chavez in Venezuela in 2002, a move that could have had dramatic consequences, leading to another civil war.

Has some decoupling already occurred by comparison with the Reagan era?

There was some calm during the Clinton administration, but the Bush administration has put Latin American policy in the hands of right-wing extremists, in a very worrisome move.

How can Colombia, Mexico, and the other countries whose politics and economics have been affected by nacrotraffic and other US influences get their civil societies back in effective action?

I wish I knew. But in any case, it starts with the reform of the state and of the military, and not being too concerned with drug exports, but with their effects on the institutions of the country.

And what about the biggest and most populous of the Latin American countries – Brazil? It is known in the outside world as a place where acute pressures are leading to deforestation

and other forms of damage, as well as to acute human exploita-
tion. But economic and political reform have been far-reaching
and the country does have a working civil society. Might it be
a testbed – by comparison with, say, China – for a consensus-
based way of building a future for a complex society?

Brazil is of course the decisive country in Latin America, and
one of the most important countries in the world, and not
only in soccer (an English sport invention made into an art
by the Brazilians). I also feel very strongly about Brazil, in
personal terms. You know, in 1968 I spent one month living
in the home of my friends Fernando Henrique and Ruth
Cardoso, in São Paulo. I always kept in close touch with
Brazil, and with Fernando Henrique and Ruth, even when he
became president. They are the only friends I have kept the
same closeness with after they became politically important.
[see conversation 1.]

Because of my personal story about Brazil, I do have my
bias. I do think Cardoso has done an exceptional job as president, by modernizing the country, killing hyperinflation, and
bringing Brazil competitively into the global economy. He
has also helped to make improvements in health and education, the two key areas of social policy. Yet Brazil remains one
of the most frustrating countries in the world. As Cardoso
said in his electoral campaign, Brazil is not an underdeveloped country, it is an unjust society. And because of this
injustice, millions remain marginal and uneducated, and the
social and environmental problems are staggering.

Brazil has a highly educated middle class, many good
professionals, a sophisticated high-tech industry, a dynamic
financial system, good telecommunications infrastructure,
after privatization, and the only competitive manufacturing
exports sector in Latin America. The University of São Paulo
produces more scientific research than the rest of Latin
America put together.

At the same time, there is a dynamic civil society, an active
community movement, a very militant labor movement,
modern globalized media, and a sophisticated intelligentsia.

But Brazil is sick from too many major problems that have not improved in the last decade, and continue to bring down the huge possibilities of the country. First, social inequality, the highest in the world, with Haiti. This inequality permeates throughout the public sector, and reproduces itself in the education system, so perpetuating the obstacles to social mobility. I do think that it is functional that the middle class, including the ideologically progressive middle class, can live very well, with plenty of servants and extraordinary privileges, such as the possibility of retiring at the age of 50 as university professors with full salary for the rest of their lives – to take another, better-paid job. Even the labor unions represent a labor aristocracy, in a country where close to 40 percent of the urban labor force is in the informal economy. Unions tend to represent workers in relatively well-paid, protected jobs, in the public sector and in the modern industries. Brazil is 81 percent urban, so rural poverty, although desperate, does not account for the bulk of social problems. So this is a society in which those who are active social actors are in fact the privileged ones, while the vast majority of the poor and marginalized are engaged in survival strategies, and become a potential support for demagogy. The lack of perspective leads to messianic religious influence, to widespread crime and violence, and to the prevalence of networks of survival, all in contrast with a very modern, globalized production and consumption segment of society.

The other major problem is the political class. There are no real parties, except, and only to some extent, the left-wing party, the PT, or Labour Party, which emerged from the cross-fertilization between the labor movement and the Catholic Church, with some of the most prominent and generous intellectuals. There is an extraordinary level of corruption and pork barrel politics, in which most politicians tend to their own interests and to serving their constituencies, with little concern for the country or for any broad political project. There are exceptions, of course – Cardoso, Lula [the PT leader at the time of writing, and later president], Marta Suplicy (the mayor of São Paulo), and a few others – but I am talking not about personalities, but about the political class and the political system.

And because Brazil is a truly federal state, the fragmentation of politics is reproduced throughout its vast geography, making it very difficult to govern the country in terms of social policies. This is why a reformist administration such as Cardoso's could act on macroeconomic matters, on infrastructure, on foreign policy, on internationally related development policies, but could do much less on issues of social reform. This would require a revamping of the institutional and political system of Brazil, and this would be resisted by the powerful vested interests entrenched in the structures of the state. Thus Brazil is an economic giant and a social disaster. The contradiction between the dynamism of its globalized sector and the desperation of its increasingly marginalized majority may reach unsustainable levels. I believe that the likely presidents of Brazil after Cardoso will be determined to tackle this issue. If they do, on the solid foundation built by Cardoso at the economic level, Brazil may become a less unjust society, and then an extraordinarily dynamic country that could pull Latin America out of underdevelopment and dependency vis-à-vis the USA.

Next I'd like to ask about Africa. In The Information Age *you were clear that its state was a global concern, one now much more widely shared than it was then. Do you agree with those who say that the example of Latin America, which has drawn back from the dictatorship and oppression of the 1970s and 1980s, is relevant to Africa? If not, is it because the problems are much worse?*

No, I do not agree, because, as you suggest, the problems are much worse. The main issue is institutions. By and large, Africa does not have reliable states, save South Africa, of course, Mozambique, and partly Uganda. States tend to be a conglomerate of personal interests and cliques, with support in ethnic groups, or alliances of ethnic and regional groups. This is much less the case in Latin America, where the construction of the nation-state since the early nineteenth century integrated most of the nation, with dominance established in terms of class interests and political ideologies, much more like in Europe. Furthermore, nationalism was critical to unify the nation in Latin America. There were certainly also ethnic differences: countries like Bolivia, Peru, Ecuador, and Guatemala have substantial indigenous populations. But the problem was dealt with by their massive exclusion from the political system and from the state, unlike in Africa, where ethnicity was the basis for political power groups.

Now, why so? There is one obvious difference: time. Africa started its independence process only in the 1950s, so states came to be formed very slowly. But I think a very major responsibility is with the West, which treated Africa as a neo-colonial ground, with the old colonial powers maintaining their spheres of influence, supporting their cronies, and the USA and the USSR jockeying for influence and position in the cold war, which ended up being more bloody in Africa than in Latin America or, of course, Europe. If we take the ultimate rape of a country by its own state, that is Zaire–Congo, Mobutu was on the payroll of the CIA, and obeyed Washington's orders. The atrocious war in Angola was a direct expression of the confrontation between the USA and the USSR/Cuba, as was Ethiopia, and therefore Eritrea, as was Somalia, and so on. So Africa came to independence late, could not take advantage of the process of globalization, because it was too weak to compete. The states were neo-colonial structures, the world powers used these countries as pawns, and the political economy of poverty was very functional for the corrupt political elites to enrich themselves and trickle down a little bit to their ethnic/regional networks of patronage. I cannot see how democracy could alter that. Democracy in the current African conditions is really a masquerade, again saving South Africa. It is a completely different matter, not only because it is a rather developed country, but because the ANC has built a rather legitimate state, with a strong public administration.

Has too much of Africa joined the Fourth World of which you write, whose inhabitants are too marginalized to be worth exploiting?

In the early 1960s Africa was in much better relative condition vis-à-vis East Asia or Latin America than it is today. The lesson is not that colonialism worked better, but that neocolonialism destroyed the institutional conditions while opening up the subsistence economies to the world market. Now the overwhelming proportion of Africans are too uneducated to be exploited as producers, in the absence of productive infrastructure, and too poor to be interesting consumers. So raw materials (including energy resources), some basic commodities, and precious and rare metals and stones are the only tradeable goods. The extraordinary potential of tourism cannot be realized under conditions of banditism, and most attempts at modernization are controlled by the corrupt elites for their own benefit.

If there was ever a situation that justified a revolution (in the strict sense – that is, the destruction of the political system and the rebuilding of the political capacity of society), it is Africa, generally speaking. The trouble is, most of the revolutions in the last decade (for example, in Congo) have killed thousands and destroyed the countries, only to end up with the same kind of political mechanism of primitive accumulation by force. It is really a human tragedy, and the West looks on from the side, and still tries to get advantage – for instance, in Liberia, where the civil war is based on the support of France for one faction and by the USA and the UK for another.

As you point out, every city in the world has its corner of the Fourth World, and every African capital has its internationally connected elites and its profitable businesses. In the latter case, the members of such elites have no incentive to get involved with the poor of their own country except perhaps to provide low-grade and low-paid labor. How can the interests of these groups be reconnected?

The members of the elites have a vested interest in keeping their people poor. First, because international aid represents a substantial proportion (sometimes the majority) of the state budget: this is what I called the political economy of poverty. Second, because if people improve their standard of living and their education, an active civil society may emerge, jeopardizing the stability of the corrupt powers. So, the notion is to be as Fourth World as possible, so as to enjoy the privileges of being the intermediaries of the First World.

Is it possible to encourage the well-off in the developed world to take an interest in Africa's problems? Or is Africa just too alien and different? Have there been too many Rwandas, Angolas, and Mozambiques for it to be regarded as part of the same planet as the rich world occupies?

The First World is fundamentally indifferent to Africa's problems. Basically, nobody cares, and many use an implicitly racist argument to justify its plight. The NGOs – some of them – do care. Others have found a good line of business in international charity. But even the best ones, such as Oxfam or Médécins sans Frontières, have tremendous difficulties in improving people's conditions because they must go through government bureaucracies, and there the problems start. Rwanda's genocide (almost half a million people massacred) was accomplished with the full knowledge of the West (Belgium and the United States, for sure), and nothing was done to stop it. It would have been easy, but nobody wanted to alter the balance of power in the area or to risk a few hundred dead soldiers. Does this tell you the real measure of Western interest in the African plight?

But, as you say, there is always hope in life. Your work in South Africa [conversation 2] has told you that at least one African government is serious about its country's role in the information age. South Africa has exceptional resources by African standards, but are they enough to make significant inroads into the exclusion from the information age which most of its citizens feel?

Well, yes, hope is cheap and easy; it would be discomforting to think about hundreds of millions of people, and their numerous descendants, sentenced to atrocious lives and early deaths for ever. So, yes, I hope that South Africa can do better. It has an advanced technological and productive structure, a very conscious population, some level of social organization, a strong popular party, the ANC, still enjoying political legitimacy, a very good political elite, highly educated and, by and large, no more corrupt than in, say, France or Italy. Mandela is still an extraordinary moral reserve. And I like Mbeki – he is a good leader and knows the world very well. And I like the finance minister, Trevor Manuel – he is committed and sophisticated, and much less neoliberal than his critics say. He just knows the conditions under which he must operate in the global economy. The problem is that South Africa has a devastating Aids epidemic, still out of control, and rising criminal violence, and apartheid has left a terrible legacy in terms of lack of education for the black population. So I think South Africa will have plenty of work to pull itself out of the disaster, and little energy and resources will be left for its leadership role for the rest of the continent.

Maybe Mozambique could be pulled out together with South Africa. But little more. Besides, the current leaders of other African countries are very distrustful of South African leadership. They would feel threatened in their privileges.

If the work you have been involved with in South Africa is a success, how would it connect to the rest of – at least sub-Saharan – Africa?

The work is still very preliminary. I cannot call it a success yet. Success does not depend on advisers, but on what the government does, and this is still limited. But if the model works, similar UN committees, in which I am also involved, could use it as a testing ground for new development policies around the continent.

If it did, how does the concept of a network society translate into societies whose economies are dominated by commodities for export?

Precisely, they are connected in what they can provide to the global network (low value-added) and disconnected in all the rest. Networks are both connection and disconnection, and this is the reality of Africa today.

Developed world movements have also put substantial effort into developing technology appropriate for Africa (mainly) and other parts of the poor world. What is the equivalent of this in the network age?

Well, if by this we mean that we need vaccines for malaria, or open source software with very simple applications for managing agricultural information, yes. If by this we mean that the Africans should specialize in Stone Age survival abilities while we speed away in the Internet age, this is a sophisticated form of elitist racism.

The sombre picture of African development has been darkened further in recent years by HIV/Aids, and by the emergence of other serious diseases from central Africa. Is the developed world's response to this crisis adequate, and can the rest of the picture improve if it is not?

Well, no, the West has refused to cooperate in providing free medicines; until recently, has been concentrating on protecting property rights, and has deformed Mbeki's argument that was, essentially, to say that Aids prevention policies in the West do not work in Africa because the level of poverty, the hygienic conditions, and the forms of sexism (my words) make Aids very specific. Without denying that some Africans have made stupid statements on the connection between the HIV virus and Aids, more has been written about this in the West than about the specific problems of Aids development in Africa – linked to women's exploitation, migration, and the lack of proper health services, not just to the virus.

*One of the developed world's most successful citizen move-
ments of recent years has been the debt relief lobby, started
mainly by churches and taken up across a wide political front.
What should the next such campaign be?*

I never say what is to be done, remember. But the debt relief
campaign shows that unreachable goals could be reached.
The world moves, even Africa, and African-related miseries.

*Next, and finally on your world tour, we arrive in Europe, my
home, yours some of the time, and the place where both ends
of this discussion are rooted for now. British people are prone
to complain that the European Union is keen to homogenize an
entire continent. By contrast, your experience as a Catalan is of
variation at a regional level becoming more important, not less,
within a European as much as a national context. Although you
probably feel little sympathy for them, could you give some
comfort to these British Eurosceptics?*

First of all, Europe and the European Union are not the same.
I do not know if there is an entity called Europe, although it
probably refers to a shared geography and history for thousands of years, with the proviso that most of this sharing
consisted in killing each other, taking advantage of relative
physical proximity. Christianity is probably also a bond, otherwise northern Africa should be included in this spatiotem-
poral area through secular violence. But if we say so, what
about Turkey, and Albania, and Bosnia, and all Muslim
minorities throughout Europe? Would they be non-Euro-
peans? And if we say Christianity, how can we make room
for the militant secularization of most European states –
France, for instance? England, of course, is a benign theocratic
monarchy, with the King or Queen as the official religious
leader of the nation, one more oddity of this exotic British
culture. You can see how difficult it is actually to define
Europe. But in any case, the geo-historical space should be
defined from the Urals (and beyond, since Siberia is demo-
graphically the most Russian of all Russian land) to Finis-
terre, and from the Arctic Circle to some borderline in the
Mediterranean.

The European Union as an institutional system will not reach this definition, because Russia is too big, and too feared by many of the European nations, to be a full member of such a union, even in the long term.

Is it possible for European countries to exist rationally outside the EU? Or is it only possible if, like Norway or Switzerland, they have very specialist economies?

There are, and will be, exceptions, such as Norway and Switzerland, Andorra, or Lichtenstein, both as expressions of irreducible identity and as functional decisions in specializing in what EU countries cannot do.

European economic union was a response to US economic success. But it is also a political project as the launch of the euro shows, as does the eastwards spread of the union since the collapse of the Iron Curtain. In our politics conversation [conversation 6] you said that it is a network organization and essentially benign. But does it in fact take power away from some groups or organizations that are used to having it?

The European Union, as an institutional system, is committed to building some new form of state. It is a very confused, pragmatic project, that was always propelled by a defensive instinct. First, it was a project against the demons of another European war; this is why it was built on a founding block, integrating France and Germany, starting with the coal and steel industries, the key industrial sectors of the old forms of war. Then this geopolitical aim was reinforced, through Nato, by building Europe against the Soviet Union. The second stage came in the 1980s, when the threat of economic and technological dependency on the USA and Japan provided the stimulus for further economic integration and technological cooperation. Then the process of globalization made it clear that an economically united Europe would stand a better chance of maneuvering in the global flows of wealth and power than each individual state. Thus, Maastricht, convergence, the EU Central Bank, and, finally, the euro, that effectively integrates the European economies (the UK will certainly join, it is just a matter of political timing).

Let's talk about Schengen Europe: freedom of movement, labor, etc. for the insiders, but no rights for anyone else. Is this system a stable base for a successful economy, or does there also have to be more tolerance of immigration and mobility? Might countries which are disinclined to befriend immigrants benefit from EU-wide initiatives which would make them do so?

Schengen came next, as a symbol of fortress Europe: opening borders within the new state, strengthening controls and boundaries vis-à-vis the outside world, so redefining the political and police space. As for workers' mobility, there are obstacles to full integration, but the trend is towards the full integration of the European labor market, at least for EU nationals.

So Europe has become a large, integrated economic space. On the other hand, it has also developed a very complex set of institutions and institutional arrangements that link up all governments, and even nongovernmental organizations. Nation-states do not disappear, they transform themselves by sharing sovereignty to win power together, rather than becoming powerless on their own. So what I call the network state characterizes the EU. It is a state made up of institutional links between EU institutions (including the EU Council made up of nation-states), national governments, regional governments, local governments, and NGOs, and extending internationally through multiple links on such important decision-making institutions as Nato, the IMF, the UN, the European Conference on Security, and a myriad of international agreements that bind the EU in trade, the environment, security, human rights, etc. This is the actual, operational state in which we live in Europe nowadays.

And it will become more complex, and with greater distance between member nation-states and the EU institutions, as new members come in, all the way up to 27 nation-states.

I think it is unlikely that this will evolve towards a federal state, because of the vested interests of the existing nation-states, and because of the strengthening of national identities. A weak European identity cannot match the influence of strong national identities. And without a dominant European identity, in a democracy, nations will not dissolve their autonomy. Rather, they will capture the European institutions as instruments of their shared sovereignty, which is the case nowadays.

Europe is a continent of many fascinating identities – but in many places these are associated with violent self-defense, as in Ireland and the former Yugoslavia on the basis of ancient religious divisions, or, as in many places, associated with more recent hostility to immigrants. Do official, national, or European initiatives to counter these "hostile" identities work, or do history and social change have to work at their own pace?

The interesting matter concerns what you call regional identities, some of which I call (historically grounded) national, such as the Catalan, the Basque, or the Scottish identity. Not only have they survived, but they are stronger every day, as a part of the general trend toward the importance of cultural identity in a globalized world. For these generally subdued identities, the European Union is a much better environment than their dominant nation-state (for example, Spain vis-à-vis Catalonia). They strive at the same time for increasing federalism inside the nation-states and for increasing federalism within the European Union, so that their level of autonomy is maximized without rupture. The equation is that European federalism, oppressed national identities, and strong local and regional identities go hand in hand in the construction of a supranational Europe, while nation-state-based national identities (still the predominant ones in Europe) block full progress towards a federal state. The outcome of this process is a variable geometry of institutions and decision-making mechanisms that I have theorized as a network state, expressing the complexity of managing global processes and specific identities from an inherited nation-state institutional system.

The real issue, then, as you say, is how you build a European identity, not to replace the historically built identities, but by overlaying them. I wrote a report for the Portuguese Presidency of the EU in 2000 on this matter. The key notion is that what is needed is a material process of constructing identity by stimulating sharing of practices that matter to people. Without a shared identity, it is not so sure that Europe can remain as an institutional construction beyond a common market. On the other hand, any imposition of an artificial identity on what people actually feel would create a backlash.

In a democratic context, Europe cannot do with national or regional identities what centuries ago France did with Brittany, England did with Ireland, or Spain did with Catalonia. This is why I think that what British people feel about Europe is very respectable, but not realistic. You cannot have a common economy, and nothing else in common. A major economic crisis would probably shatter the institutional basis of common management, if there is not some kind of feeling of belonging. The trick is to find ways to accommodate identity and autonomy with an overlaid identity related to common instrumentality in European institutions, reinforced by a boundary of Europeanness vis-à-vis the rest of the world, not based on religion or race. For this, the British people must accept the price of lower autonomy in exchange for greater wealth. And the key to this is not so much to lose independence as to sever the critical link with the United States. The real distinctive line of European identity is vis-à-vis America. Europeanness without a clear distinction in regard to America would be a suspicious, Western, ethnic statement.

I do feel European, Catalan, and Spanish (though I am not proud of Spanish history – I am even ashamed, I would say, of what the Spanish state did). I think it is a great feeling to create conditions to make it more difficult to kill each other, knowing that if people and societies still want to kill, they will have plenty of opportunity to do it in other places.

Besides, yes, European institutions may be more prone to be open to immigrants and multiculturalism than national or local ones, in a similar vein to what happens in the USA, where the federal government is usually more receptive to the interests of minorities.

Then the issue of a more assertive European foreign policy. The UK at least is very clear in this matter: UK foreign policy is often US foreign policy with a human face. EU foreign policy certainly has a human face, but has tremendous difficulty becoming effective, even though the main actor in this policy, Javier Solana, is, in my personal assessment, one of the most able and honest political leaders in the world. But the EU is too contradictory, too diverse, and too indecisive to have a unified foreign policy. This is the price for not being a federal state. Furthermore, there is a very hypocritical attitude among the Europeans: they claim independence from the USA, yet they are not ready to foot the bill or to build a credible defense force. The wars in the Balkans showed Europe's inability to solve its own problems. The terrorist threat is more directly targeted at the USA, but Europe is not immune. Yet, while some governments, particularly the UK, took the matter seriously, most Europeans blame the Americans as imperialists. I am certainly critical of the foreign policy of the Bush administration, and I think it is a fundamentally wrong strategy to solve the problems of the world by bombing without information. However, if Europe wants a different world from the one resulting from the exercise of global power by the USA, it has to accept the price for it: the economic price, the military price, and the price of making tough decisions and implementing them.

Why does Europe's economic success not lead to more cultural self-confidence? For example, what is behind the European snobbery about Hollywood?

Absolutely. The cultural exception, à la France, is a self-defeating policy. Europe is rich enough, and has enough of a market, to compete in market terms with US media production. The problem is that most European creators do not accept the commercialization of their products. This is all right, but then they should not expect to go beyond the small circles of cultural elites. There is professionalism in Hollywood production that is highly diversified, not just stupid action movies or soap operas. The key is to enhance the quality of what Europeans do in media, in television, in music. Because, after all, many of the creators working in California are from Europe. So the dismantling of European protectionism and of the European art cliques (in many cases mediocrity protected by nationalism) is a precondition for the young creators to be able to do their job in Europe. So what you call snobbery towards Hollywood is in fact the vested interests of old boy networks capturing public subsidies and protectionist legislation because they cannot compete in and with America. Because most people in Europe do prefer American movies or, for that matter, anything that is technically good, in each genre, regardless of its origin.

And why is Europe such a poor developer of new intellectual content – on calculations of Nobel prize winners, major new companies (with exceptions such as Airbus), etc.?

Well, as you say, there are very good scientists in Europe, important technological innovations, and some major commercial breakthroughs. Not only Airbus (a major one), but mobile telecommunications, and, soon, the wireless Internet. Besides, many European hackers (particularly in Finland and the Netherlands) are at the forefront of innovation. So I see Europe reversing its technological and entrepreneurial lag vis-à-vis the United States, although in overall economic competitiveness, statistics show the gap has been increasing in the last five years, after the explosion of the new economy in the USA. I think there are two fundamental differences with the USA. The first one, and the most fundamental, is the university system. The leading American research universities are without parallel in Europe. Only a handful of UK universities are in the same league, and not among the first group. The only reason I moved to the USA 23 years ago was because I could not do in Europe the research I could do in the USA. I could never have written my trilogy from Paris or Madrid. The combination of flexible institutions, openness to the world, excellent libraries, research climate, and, above all, outstanding graduate students in real doctoral programs creates the kind of environment that is decisive for scholarship, science, and technology. It just happens that science, technology, and knowledge are the source of wealth and power in our world. And universities are the institutions that produce this, and the holders of this knowledge. This is the real superiority of the USA. Everything else follows.

On the other hand, the institutional environment for business makes possible the development of entrepreneurialism and innovation, the keys for productivity and competitiveness. I mean issues such as flexible regulations, flexible capital, and labor markets, the existence of an agile venture capital network able to finance innovation, open immigration policy, and the like. Under such conditions the huge social problems in the USA, and the pitiful state of public services, including education and health, become a hazard, but cannot forestall the dynamism that results from knowledge, entrepreneurialism, flexible capital, and flexible labor. This is the current debate in European policymaking circles. But unless Europe reforms its university system, it will be dependent on the USA for the essential factor in wealth and power: the autonomous capacity to generate knowledge.

Parts of Europe – especially in Eastern Europe but also, say, areas of most British, Italian, or French cities – are part of the Fourth World. Does the sort of successful city regeneration you write about (and showed me in Barcelona) translate to other places, or is it very particular, so that each case of urban crisis needs a unique solution?

In fact, here European cities are much better off than the rest of the world, in spite of pockets of poverty. Barcelona is a role model because it brings together modernity, competitiveness, and social welfare with cultural heritage, artistic creativity, architectural innovation, and civic culture. It is an example of the culture of cities renewed under the conditions of the information age. But there are many other examples of cities developing along a similar trajectory: Birmingham, Stockholm, Amsterdam, and to some extent Berlin, among others. The problem is the peripheries of many cities, particularly in France and in England, with ethnic ghettos of poverty and unemployment gradually being taken over by the criminal culture.

Barcelona, and others, are doing better in this regard, but there are problems. Europe needs to accept its multiethnic reality, and also tackle issues of urban marginality with locally tailored programs, together with the residents, learning more from America not in urban development in general (in this sense, European cities are much better off), but from American programs targeting urban poverty. The European welfare state is too generic, and is not flexible enough to adapt to local conditions. A local welfare state is much needed, combining social policies and urban planning.

Do you believe that WTO-type measures to impose uniform standards of competitiveness and openness on economic activity menace the continental model of the mixed economy and state participation in industry? Or will ways be found around it?

I think Europe does have a competitive advantage by keeping (while modernizing) the welfare state: the production of a better labor force, social stability, creation of a wide market for public services, etc. Remember, the Finnish model, based on a combination of technological innovation and the welfare state, made Finland the most competitive economy in the world. But this is not a mixed economy model: it is a market economy and a publicly protected society.

Do you expect to live in Europe, full- or part-time, again?

Yes, from now on, I will stay and finish my life in Barcelona. However, I will still be lecturing and researching around the world, and keeping my attachment to Berkeley and other major universities. My way of life has always been local and global at the same time, and I suspect this has become a structural feature of my personality.

Conversation 8

A World of Knowledge

MARTIN INCE   *The world you describe is above all one which is dense in information. It differs from the world of a few decades ago mainly because of the skein of data flowing between points all over the world and influencing what we do. The most important and high-value work is done by experts in the use of information. The most important new projects are essentially about data – for example, as we said in conversation 2, the genomics and biotechnology nexus is essentially an outgrowth of the IT industry.*

   How would you describe the distinction between data, information, knowledge, and something even more high-level, wisdom and judgment? Is it possible with modern technology, especially knowledge-management software, for the process of getting from data to its use to be truncated and automated?

MANUEL CASTELLS   Information is an organized data set, formatted for communication purposes, on the basis of some principle of classification (although sometimes the origins of the classification principle are forgotten). Knowledge is the set of statements that result from applying the human mind to understanding an observable phenomenon, and is obtained by using the scientific procedures determined as scientific by the scientific community in a given historical context. Wisdom and judgment are systems of evaluation and decision making that take place in the human mind on the basis of the interaction between knowledge, personal experience, cultural values, and the personality of the human being holding the wisdom and effectuating the judgment. Computers cannot make judgments outside their programs, and they definitely cannot exercise wisdom, since they do not have personal experience, cultural values, or personality.

But we must consider how much the recurrent interaction between computers' programmed decisions and the feedback from their environment can influence future programs, thus modifying the information base and, with it, the knowledge base for decision. In other words, is there self-evolving programming capability? Unless we go into science fiction, this does not seem to be the case nowadays. However, there is co-evolution between the human brain and the computer, learning from each other, but learning from an individual human brain, so that the co-evolution is always specific to a given personality system. So a computer cannot become a subject in its own right, but I could have (actually my grandchildren may have) a computer as an extension of the mind, whose reactions and help affect the mind, inducing individualized co-evolution between people and their machines. So knowledge-management software is a low-level application for routine operations that can be truncated and distributed, but cannot respond to an evolving context, where the critical decisions have to be made.

But there is new software emerging that allows this specific co-evolution, providing to a given individual, in real time, the data (stored knowledge) needed for her decisions, and allowing for a recurrent feedback that amplifies her capacity at managing her environment.

One of the possible criticisms of the world of weightless industry and constant flow is that data spends a lot of time being transmitted (as do people) from place to place, but its generation is less closely analyzed.

My analysis is in direct contradiction to the notion of the weightless economy. The studies on Internet companies show exactly that they are always a hybrid of physical infrastructure and information flows. Amazon would be nothing without UPS, and both need huge warehouses and a fleet of planes. The problem is that futurologists have polluted our understanding with fantasy projections of the Internet-based world. The world is indeed based on the Internet, but geography, history, and institutions do not disappear: places are networked, people are networked, companies are networked, and states are still based on their capacity to obliterate their enemies by bombing them with explosives. However, without information, you do not know what, whom, or where to bomb. Without knowledge and information, the best industrial plant in the world cannot effectively produce and sell. So what is fundamental is that connectivity and knowledge are the higher value-generating activities, but there is no value that can be disembodied from the material world. In fact, the material world embodies information and knowledge, and this is how and why the Internet is important: it connects materiality and symbol processing.

What do you think of as the main sources of information in the information age?

Who generates knowledge and information? Well, knowledge is very clear: universities and research centers around the world, most of them public research centers, but also major research centers of some corporations, and innovative units of technological entrepreneurs. There are still some traditional forms of knowledge generation, such as indigenous people knowing the curative virtues of some plants in their environment, or the meditation capacity of some individuals in some cultures. However, the share of traditional knowledge in the total stock of knowledge dwindles every day. So one should not reject these forms of knowledge, that sometimes are precious, but what characterizes our Information Age is precisely the ability to bring all these data into a common system, and process them at a higher level of sophistication.

Knowledge generation and its public diffusion are essential for the well-being of our species. This is why intellectual property rights are the main enemy of human progress, although they are going to make thousands of lawyers rich around the world. Now, the real change is where information comes from. Information in the Internet age comes from people, people producing their information and exchanging it over the net. This is the true revolution. We do not have too much information (as we do not have too many books in a library, just more options to find the one we really want). It is the endless collective capacity of society to produce its own information, to distribute it, to recombine it, to use it for its specific goals, that transforms social practice, through the transformation of the range of possibilities for the human mind.

Scientific projects generate gigabytes of data every day – the original rationale for the web. The ability to produce it and, more importantly, to make sense of it has altered intellectual life fundamentally. Is something analogous happening in the rest of the world of knowledge? In politics, always so greedy for new information? Or in the business world? In the 1960s 50s *the UK got a second TV channel, and there was serious doubt about whether there would be enough material to fill it. How do people make sense of thousands of channels?*

Making sense of knowledge has always been the decisive operation, and the source of wealth and power. But this is also knowledge. In other words, knowledge does not come in packages: it is generated by applying knowledge to process information, to act upon people and their environment. So, to know what to know and how to know it and what to do with it is the most decisive form of knowledge. This is why the social sciences are the most important form of scientific knowledge, because they even condition how the "hard sciences'" knowledge can be generated. The problem is that social sciences are in a most primitive state (and enjoying it – it's much less work) and are permeated by ideology in the process itself. All sciences live in ideology, but natural sciences learned a long time ago to keep ideology at a distance from the hard core of their experimentation procedures – that is what created modern science.

Do you think that making sense of knowledge has become more important than producing it? Is its production often a routine task which is done by poorly-paid staff on an industrial basis, while its interpretation is more interesting and better rewarded?

Now, production – for instance, industrial production – does not necessarily have to be a routine task. In fact, routine tasks can be better done by machines. Translating knowledge (through technology) into material production is not only essential, for obvious reasons, but the quality of the process and of the product will be decisive in the marketplace, and this quality can only be achieved by knowledge application in the production process. Yet, most added value depends on how much knowledge is embodied in products and services.

You think that the equipment used to transmit information around the world is not too interesting. In The Information Age *you even claim that the launching of satellites is more or less a routine, low-value industrial activity, although "Rocket Science" has entered the language as a term for something that is very demanding. As a social scientist rather than an electrical engineer, your take on it seems to be that the infrastructure for the information age will find its way everywhere it needs to be, on a basis decided politically, economically, and on business grounds. Is this true? Or is there a role for newer technology that would lower costs, enhance performance, and make the information age more accessible to more people? If so, would that mean further power shifts and enable more novel forms of organization to flourish?*

You are right on the critical importance of technological infrastructure. My remark on satellite launching really tries to shift the priority to a different world, the world of nano-technology, of genetic engineering, of sensor-based interacting software, of brain-adaptive interface software, of bioelectronic materials, that is the real cutting edge of the scientific and technological frontier (together with social sciences, as I said – but this is the frontier for the twenty-second century . . .).

In fact, I am personally committed, with the UN, with South Africa, and in other contexts, to favoring the building of a technological communications infrastructure in the developing world, as we discussed in conversation 2, without which it is impossible to ensure any process of development. But it must be a multidimensional process, developing in harmony the information and communications infrastructure, the human resources to manage it, and the specific applications to be developed for the needs and values of each country.

These specific applications would imply new forms of technological development, adapted to social uses and to lower levels of income. The way to expand technology markets is to include in the market technology tools for uses that are currently not expressed in the market. Public spending, or donors' spending, could pump-prime these new markets, so that new technological forms could emerge. It is the old problem of spending huge amounts of money on cancer research, and very little on finding vaccines for the relatively simple illnesses that devastate the Third World. Even cheap ICT goods and services, if they could tap a market of billions of people at a very low price, could be good both for people and for companies. In other words, the social basis of economic accumulation must be expanded for new forms of technological development to flourish. And with them, yes, new organizational forms and a power shift.

You have spent your adult life in universities. The oldest of these still in business in Europe date from the Middle Ages. As you know, I work some of the time on a newspaper for the UK university sector. We often get people asking why the lecture, that most traditional of university methodologies, survived the arrival of video technology and the Internet. But we recently got a letter asking why lectures even survived the invention of printing. What is the intellectual and organizational future of universities?

Universities combine, and have combined throughout history and with various emphases, four main functions: ideological apparatuses (originally theological schools), institutions for elite selection and social stratification in society, training systems for producing labor with proper skills, and knowledge-generating factories. The major research university tends to combine all of these functions, with emphasis on the production of knowledge. Business schools focus on the production of good managers, together with the creation of cultural milieus for the networks of future managers. The Oxbridges of the world continue to function mainly as elite selection systems, rooted in ideological traditions, although they certainly train students for work and produce knowledge (in fact, more than the average European university).

The ability of university systems to combine all these functions is the critical matter for their survival and growth. They do not necessarily have to be integrated in one and the same university. Differentiation of the system, while making bridges possible between different universities and schools, ensures flexiblity and, ultimately, productivity for economy and society at large. The more a university is oriented towards knowledge production, the more it needs to be flexible and to provide general training, rather than specific specialization in some skills, because specific skills become rapidly obsolete.

Large companies often cite "IT skills," "literacy" and "numeracy," rather than knowledge of anything specific as their main demand in the graduates they hire. Is this because knowledge is so fast-growing in the Information Age that the ability to get new skills is more vital that any actual knowledge?

In the knowledge economy, in the Information Society, the fundamental matter is to learn throughout the whole life cycle. That is because information is on the net; the key is to have the capacity to know what information to look for, to retrieve this information and to recombine it, applying it to the specific tasks and projects we have in each moment of our life, and for each context.

You divide work initially into two broad categories, generic and specialized. How solid is this distinction?

Self-programmable people are those who can reprogram themselves throughout their life. "Generic" means that anyone is indistinguishable from another pair of arms or, for that matter, from a robot. Now, universities are in the business of producing self-programmable labor, and in the updating and upgrading of this labor throughout the life cycle.

This is where on-line education becomes essential. For young students entering life, a good, traditional college campus is essential, albeit a number of courses and learning processes can be part of their training, because this will broaden the stock of information and knowledge they can have access to. But for people already engaged in their professional life, already with families, but still in need of recycling themselves, of acquiring new knowledge, of getting higher degrees, of changing their professional projects, then on-line education is the privileged tool. Not just as *ad hoc* vocational programs, but via full-fledged, degree-granting universities. The Open University of Catalonia (UOC) is a high-quality institution of higher education, granting the same degrees as other Catalan universities, to a student body (in Catalonia and around the world), 80 percent of which works full-time, and logs in at their convenience. I see this kind of education as fitting the needs of developing countries that cannot wait to reproduce a quality university system on a mass scale following the nineteenth-century model of European or American universities.

Another role which universities have in modern societies is as the driver of new economic development. Your own institution, Berkeley, is known worldwide as one of the founders of Silicon Valley, and governments far and wide would like to know how to imitate it.

The role of universities in economic development is essential, but does not always impact their immediate regional environment. By the way, Berkeley was not at the origin of Silicon Valley, Stanford was (besides beating us regularly in sports). And it was so because Berkeley always looked down on the business implications of its great science, while Stanford actively promoted business investment, and supported its faculty and students in this task [Conversation 2]. Yet, Berkeley, and other major research universities in the USA, were and are critical as producers of knowledge, of scientists, of innovators – the stuff of which the information technology revolution and the new economy are made. Some decisive software, in open source, came out of Berkeley, and some of the most important breakthroughs in genetic engineering came from the University of California at San Francisco. These discoveries are of immense importance for the creation of wealth, through mechanisms of diffusion that follow market mechanisms or public policy initiatives, depending on institutional contexts.

Is one role for universities to do things that risk being unpopular with funders, politicians, and the powerful in general? If so, do they need to be better than they are at ignoring, perhaps at some peril, people whom their work annoys?

The unique role of the university is its independence. Only in the university can researchers be free, and only from freedom of thought can science and culture develop in the long term. And the protection of this independence is rooted in ideology, tradition, and networks of social protection by the university-originated elites.

There is one fundamental feature common to all good universities: they are independent of the directly exercised power of governments or private interests. In fact, universities are the last, and only, space of relative freedom, where people can think independently, research independently, and, if they are ready to live modest lives, research with very few resources in most fields. This independence is rooted in the institutions of governance and in the practice of life tenure for faculty. Take this freedom away, submit universities to the market logic, or to the commands of government, and you will kill the source of scientific, technological, and cultural innovation in our societies. In fact, most business understands this very well, and supports the autonomy of universities, because they can benefit from the openness that characterizes university research.

Without freedom in the university there would not have been the Internet, advanced computing, or genetic engineering. It's only petty business that tries to penetrate one of the last areas not submitted to a commercial logic, because speculators do not care about the consequences of their shortsighted strategy for society at large. Here is where the ideology of tradition and the role of universities as elite producers saves them, in the last resort, from being swallowed by bureaucrats and speculators. Yes, there is a great deal of corporatism, and routine, in the daily practice of the university world. But in the same way that political corruption does not justify us giving up on political democracy, so the cultural conservativism of universities and their aristocratic elitism (particularly irritating in its leftist version) does not constitute a sufficient argument to downgrade them into human resource departments of the corporate world.

The British government has a target of 50 percent participation in higher education, and other countries have similar ambitious aims. What is happening here? Is society so much more complex that we need more people with higher-grade skills and knowledge to keep the show on the road, be they nurses, soldiers, or engineers? Or have qualifications become a piece of colorful plumage that people need to take seriously as evidence of the ability to cope with complex concepts? Under such conditions, should everybody be educated in the university system?

Absolutely yes, not 50 percent, but 100 percent. Why not? We need educated people at all levels of society and in all functions of the economy. Take the fastest-growing occupation in the world: security agents, particularly in private security firms. Well, before giving someone a gun, one should be sure that she or he has the proper psychological and legal training, the proper understanding of situations, besides physical and mental fitness. The point is that we are prisoners of our traditional model, that people go to university in their young age and then go into real life, and that's it. If people, as they already do in California, go in and out of the university system, and into their professional and personal lives, at one point in time for a given age cohort, the majority may not be in the university, but at the end of the life of this cohort, maybe most of them could have been in the university at some point. This is likely to make them better people, better workers, and more informed citizens. So, rather than considering the university as the platform for our training in our young age, we could rethink it as an institution accompanying us, for different purposes, all our life. And systematically integrate it into the economy and society as the factory of knowledge and information supporting everything we do.

Given the connection between universities and economic success, is the dearth of academic resources in the developing world one of the key barriers to its progress? If so, can new technology do anything about it? For example, there are more Ethiopian academics in the USA than in Ethiopia. The number about adds up to the academic staff of a reasonable-sized university. Ethiopia cannot afford this loss. It also cannot afford to repatriate these people even if they wanted to come. Other more affluent nations such as Ireland, which are major producers of skilled emigrants, are looking at ways of reconnecting those diasporas to their homeland. Might networks help here, or is there just too strong a link between physical presence and effective learning?

The lack of quality universities in most developing countries is the main obstacle to their development. This situation is not only a matter of material resources, but also of lack of independence vis-à-vis government, the churches, and interest groups. I cannot see a more important development policy than the one oriented towards building a modern, efficient, clean, legitimate, and free university system. Networks of academics who have migrated to advanced countries' universities would be essential in helping the systems to be reformed back home. Not necessarily by returning for good, but by spending time and effort in their home countries, inspiring the new generations, and helping to create a brain circulation between different universities in the world, both physical and on-line. Networks are key to transforming globalization into a dynamic system of opportunities and synergy creation.

But universities are not alone as producers of new knowledge. The world of think tanks in the production of political, social, and economic thinking has been growing apace. Even expensive science is done by charities and in profit-making organizations as well as in universities. What is the unique role of the university?

The biggest gap in knowledge in our societies is precisely the excessive fragmentation and specialization of knowledge, and its encapsulation in bureaucratically defined disciplines. These disciplines are not defined in the terms of the real dynamics of current science. They are the result of treaties fixing the boundaries after cruel wars between academic gangs defending or conquering their turf. But, as with all boundaries in a fast-moving world (the world of knowledge generation), they become both obsolete in terms of content and essential in preserving vested interests. Thus, interdisciplinary research becomes essential as a tool of discovery. Thus, science makes progress in the cracks of institutional systems, in minor units or departments, such as city and regional planning in my case (I would certainly abstain from doing any city or regional planning – it would be irresponsible on my part); or computer science 50 years ago, a marginal unit of the sturdy engineering schools; or plant biology, a second-class citizen in the traditional biology centers; or communication and broadcasting departments, where the real social knowledge of the uses of the Internet is developing today; while sociologists spend their time rereading Durkheim and deconstructing Marx.

It is true, however, that serious scientific work needs to make incremental progress by doing painstaking empirical research focusing on one narrow segment of knowledge and expanding it. Thus, highly focused experimental research continues to be the heart of science. However, the best science combines experiments with an integrated body of knowledge across disciplinary boundaries, using this framework to inform experimental research and organizing the feedback of experimental results into the overall body of knowledge. But the theory of the magic bullet in research, with its extraordinary rewards in honors and money, tends to bias the effort towards fragments of research conducted by a team of graduate students around a narrow focus defined by their faculty adviser, in competition with other colleagues. As a result of individualization and fragmentation, in a horse race to reap the benefits of being prime mover, synthetic elaboration of what we know has been relegated to the realm of philosophical ruminations by emeritus professors. A pity. Most young faculty are discouraged from engaging in comprehensive analysis, and those who want to do "theory" are assigned to one particular area that consists in reading and commenting on the writings of conveniently dead theorists, or those who become Parisian chic fashionable objects.

Finally, I would like to finish the book with some thoughts about your own work and its importance. It is often said that since about the middle of the nineteenth century it has been impossible for anyone to have a command of the whole of knowledge. But your work has probably come closer than most in recent years to displaying an understanding of the complete realm of knowledge, apart from the outer reaches of science and theory, and further, of being based in genuine research-based understanding.

As for my own work as presented in my trilogy, you are aware of my distance from the worldwide, broad expression of interest that it has triggered. Naturally, I like to see that 15 years of effort (1984–99 for the second edition) resulted in a book that arouses some interest, that is not a useless waste of my life.

But that trilogy has entered its second edition (albeit with one volume unchanged), which suggests that even vast sweeping insights are perishable. What has the history of those books taught you about the way people get and use knowledge?

As you know, I wrote this book as my intellectual testament when I thought (with some good information in hand) that my life was about to end. So I tried to put together, in a form as coherent as possible, everything I knew about everything, without limits, but with care, since these were my last words, and the superior values in my mind are the intellectual and academic values: truth, rigor, uncompromising search for excellence. I had no target, no wish, and no discipline to worship, Ni Dieu ni Maître, in my work (in my intimate life I do believe in some kind of spiritual force). So I brought in information from many areas and from many corners, to give it away, to leave this world light of baggage.

However, the limits of my knowledge and experience are really many, and therefore erudition should not be the main contribution of my work. What I really tried to do was to find the key threads of social change in the society I saw emerging worldwide, and to propose a style of analysis and some conceptual tools that could serve to understand this process of change in the future. Not by studying the future (it cannot be done in science), but by proposing an empirically grounded analysis of the present and recent past (what started as the present in 1984 became recent past in the mid-1990s). And I wanted to do so from a multicultural perspective, and from many countries, because I had traveled so much, lived and committed deeply in so many societies, that I wanted to relate to all the people I have known around the world. I wanted my analysis to serve people in Catalonia and in California, in Russia and in France, in Chile and in Quebec, in China and in Japan. For this I needed to find a nucleus common to this multidimensional transformation and to all these contexts. I think I found it. It is not technology, in fact, although the technological transformation is the driver of all this change, and was my very useful entry point. It is the double logic of networks and identity. On the one hand, networks of instrumentality, powered by new information technologies. On the other hand, the power of identity, anchoring people's minds in their history, geography, and cultures. In between lies the crisis of institutions and the painful process of their reconstruction.

This, I believe, is the story of our historical transition to a new social landscape. And because many people do not understand their world, and find some echoes of what they feel in the hesitant words I dared to speak (because I was on my way out), they seem to relate to my work. They do not have to agree with my analysis, but they recognize the themes of what they live. At least, this is my own reading of the unsuspected echo of my testament, seen from the vantage point of my extended term of life.

Bibliography, 1967–2002 (in Reverse Chrononological Order)

I. Books (cited in the language of original publication)

A. Author or main author

2001 *The Internet Galaxy, Reflections on the Internet, Business, and Society*. Oxford: Oxford University Press. (Translated into Spanish by Plaza and Janes, French by Fayard, Catalan by Rosa dels Vents, Italian by Feltrinelli, German by Leske and Budrich; in process of translation (2002) into Swedish, Polish, Dutch, Danish, Portuguese, Korean, and Chinese.)

1996–2000 *The Information Age: Economy, Society, and Culture*. Oxford and Cambridge, MA: Blackwell.
Volume I: *The Rise of the Network Society* (1996; 2nd edn 2000).
Volume II: *The Power of Identity* (1997).
Volume III: *End of Millennium* (1998; 2nd edn 2000).
(The three volumes have been translated into Spanish (Alianza Editorial, Madrid, and Siglo XXI, Mexico), French (Fayard), Chinese (CTCC, Beijing, and Tonsan, Taipei), Portuguese (Paz e Terra, São Paulo, and Gulbenkian, Lisbon), Russian (Higher School of Economics Press), Swedish (Daedalus), Korean (Hansul), Japanese (Toshindo), Croatian, Bulgarian, Turkish, German (Leske and Budrich), Italian (EGEA/Edizioni Bocconi), Danish, Romanian, Lithuanian, Arabic, Parsi).

1999 *Global Economy, Information Society, Cities, and Regions*. Tokyo: Aoki Shoten (Published only in Japanese).

1990 *The Shek Kip Mei Syndrome. Economic Development and Public Housing in Hong Kong and Singapore.* London: Pion.

1989 *The Informational City. Information Technology, Economic Restructuring and the Urban-Regional Process.* Oxford and Cambridge, MA: Blackwell.
(Translated into Spanish (Alianza), Japanese, Chinese, and Korean.)

1986 *Nuevas tecnologías, economía y sociedad en España,* 2 vols. Madrid: Alianza Editorial.

1983 *The City and the Grassroots. A Cross-Cultural Theory of Urban Social Movements.* Berkeley: University of California Press and London: Edward Arnold. (Winner of the C. Wright Mills Award.)
(Translated into Spanish (Alianza), Japanese (Honsei University Press), and partially translated into Korean.)

1982 *Capital multinacional, estados nacionales y comunidades locales.* Mexico: Siglo XXI.

1981 *Crisis urbana y cambio social.* Madrid and Mexico: Siglo XXI.

1980 *The Economic Crisis and American Society.* Princeton, NJ: Princeton University Press and Oxford: Blackwell.
(Translated into French (Presses Universitaires de France), Spanish (Barcelona: Laia), and Chinese (Shanghai and Taipei).)

1978 a. *City, Class, and Power.* London: Macmillan and New York: St Martin's Press.
(Translated into Japanese.)
b. *Crise du logement et mouvements sociaux urbains. Enquête sur la région parisienne.* Paris: Mouton.
(Partially translated into Italian.)

1975 *Sociologie de l'espace industriel.* Paris: Anthropos.
(Translated into Spanish.)

1974 *Monopolville. L'entreprise, l'état, l'urbain.* Paris: Mouton.

1973 *Luttes urbaines.* Paris: François Maspéro.
(Translated into Spanish, Italian, German, Portuguese, and Greek.)

1972 *La Question urbaine.* Paris: François Maspéro. Revised edition; Paris: La Découverte, 1980.
(Translated into English (MIT Press and Edward Arnold, 1977), Spanish, Italian, German, Portuguese, Greek, Polish, and Japanese.)

1971   *Problemas de investigación en sociología urbana.* Madrid and Mexico: Siglo XXI.
        (Translated into Portuguese.)

B. Co-authored books

2002   *The Information Society and the Welfare State. The Finnish Model* (with Pekka Himanen). Oxford: Oxford University Press.
        (Translated into Finnish, Spanish, Catalan, and Russian.)
1997   *Local and Global. The Management of Cities in the Information Age* (with Jordi Borja). London: Earthscan.
        (Translated into Spanish.)
1995   *The Collapse of Soviet Communism: A View from the Information Society* International and Area Studies Book Series. (Berkeley: University of California Press, with Emma Kiselyova).
1994   *Technopoles of the World. The Making of 21st Century Industrial Complexes* (with Peter Hall). London and New York: Routledge.
        (Translated into Spanish (Alianza) and Chinese.)
1993   *The New Global Economy in the Information Age* (with M. Carnoy, S. Cohen, F. H. Cardoso). University Park, PA: Penn State University Press.
1992   *España, fin de siglo* (with C. A. Zaldívar). Madrid: Alianza Editorial.
        (Translated into English as *Spain beyond Myths* (Madrid: Alianza Editorial).)
1975   a. *Metodología y epistemología de las ciencias sociales* (with E. de Ipola). Madrid: Ayuso.
        b. *Participación y cambio social en la problemática contemporánea.* Buenos Aires: Sociedad Interamericana de Planificación.
1973   *La Rénovation urbaine à Paris.* Paris: Mouton.

C. Books edited or co-edited

2002   *Muslim Europe.* Washington, DC: Lexington Books (co-edited with Nezar Al-Sayyad).
1994   *Estrategias para la reindustrialización de Asturias.* Madrid: Editorial Civitas.

1992 *Andalucía: Innovación tecnológica y desarrollo económico.* Madrid: Espasa-Calpe.
1991 a. *Dual City: Restructuring New York.* New York: Russell Sage.
b. *La industria de las tecnologías de información: España en el contexto mundial (1985–1990).* Madrid: Fundesco.
c. *Las grandes ciudades en la década de los noventa.* Madrid: Sistema.
1989 *The Informal Economy. Studies in Advanced and Less Developed Countries.* Baltimore: Johns Hopkins University Press.
1986 *Territorial Development and Global Restructuring.* London: Sage.
1985 *High Technology, Space, and Society.* Beverly Hills, CA: Sage.
1974 *Estructura de clase y política urbana en América Latina.* Buenos Aires: Sociedad Interamericana de Planificación.

D. Books on Manuel Castells's research

Susser, Ida (ed.), *The Castells Reader on Cities and Social Theory.* Oxford and Malden, MA: Blackwell, 2001. (Translated into Spanish as *La sociología urbana de Manuel Castells* (Alianza Editorial).)
Muller, Johan, Cloete, Nico, and Badat, Shireen (eds), *Challenges of Globalisation: South African Debates with Manuel Castells.* Cape Town: Maskew Miller Longman, 2001.
Ince, Martin, *Conversations with Manuel Castells.* Cambridge: Polity, 2003.
Calderón, Fernando (ed.), "La era de la información en América Latina. Reflexiones con Manuel Castells" (forthcoming).
Webster, Frank (ed.), "Critiques of Manuel Castells", 3 vols, London: Sage (forthcoming).

II. Articles, essays, and book chapters

2002 "Space of Flows, Space of Places. Elements for a Theory of Urbanism in the Information Age." In Bish Sanyal (ed.), *Planning in Comparative Perspective*, Cambridge, MA: MIT Press.

2001 "Urban Sociology in the 21st Century." In Ida Susser (ed.), *The Castells Reader on Cities and Social Theory*, Oxford and Malden, MA: Blackwell, 390–406.
"Informationalism and the Network Society." Epilogue to Pekka Himanen, *The Hacker Ethic and the Spirit of Informationalism*, New York: Random House, 155–78.
"Globalization, the Knowledge Society and the Network State: Poulantzas at the Millennium" (with Martin Carnoy). *Global Networks*, 1, 1 (January): 1–18.

2000 "Materials for an Exploratory Theory of the Network Society." *British Journal of Sociology*, 51, 1 (January/March): 5–24.
"Information Technology and Global Capitalism." In Will Hutton and Anthony Giddens (eds), *On the Edge. Living with Global Capitalism*, London: Jonathan Cape and New York: The New Press, 52–74. (Translated into Spanish (Tusquets).)
"Globalización, estado y sociedad civil: el nuevo contexto histórico de los derechos humanos." *Isegoria*, 22: 5–17.
"Russia in the Information Age" (with E. Kiselyova). Paper read at Stanford University Conference on Russia at the end of the Twentieth Century, November 1999. In Victoria Bonnell and George Breslauer (eds), *Russia at the End of the 20th Century* (Translated into Russian (MIR, 2, 2001).)
"Russian Federalism and Siberian Regionalism, 1990–2000" (with E. Kiselyova). *City*, June.

1999 "Grassrooting the Space of Flows." *Urban Geography*, 20, 4 (May–June): 294–302.
The Culture of Cities in the Information Age. Paper read at the Conference on *Frontiers of the Mind in the 21st Century* organized by the US Library of Congress, June 1999. (Included in Ida Susser (ed.), *Castells Reader*, 367–89.)
"The Social Implications of Information and Communication Technologies." In *World Social Science Report*, Paris: Unesco, 236–46.

1998 "The Informational City is a Dual City. Can It Be Reversed?." In Don Schon et al. (eds), *Information Technology and Low-Income Communities*, Cambridge, MA: MIT Press, 25–42.

"The Real Crisis of Silicon Valley: A Retrospective Perspective." *Competition and Change*, 2.

1997   "Globalization, Flows, and Identity: The New Challenges of Design." In William Saunders (ed.), *Architectural Practices in the Nineties*, Princeton, NJ: Princeton Architectural Press in New York City.

1996   "The Net and the Self. Working Notes for a Critical Theory of the Informational society." *Critique of Anthropology*, 16, 1: 9–38.

"Insurgents against the New Global Order: A Comparative Analysis of Mexico's Zapatistas, the American Militia, and Japan's Aum Shinrikyo" (with S. Yazawa and E. Kiselyova). *Berkeley Journal of Sociology* (Fall).

1995   "Les flux, les réseaux et les identités: où sont les sujets dans la société informationnelle?." In François Dubet and Michel Wieviorka (eds), *Penser le sujet*, Paris: Fayard.

1994   "Paths towards the Informational Society: Employment Structure in G-7 Countries, 1920–1990" (with Yuko Aoyama). *International Labour Review*, 133, 1: 1–33.

"L'École française de sociologie urbaine vingt ans après: retour au futur?." *Les Annales de la Recherche Urbaine*, special issue (October).

"Flujos, redes e identidades." In collective author, *Nuevas perspectivas críticas en educación*, Barcelona: Paidos, 15–53.

1993   "Sociología de la crisis política rusa." *Política Exterior*, 7, 32: 55–80.

"European Cities, the Informational Society, and the Global Economy." *Journal of Economic and Social Geography*, 84, 4: 247–57. (Also published by University of Amsterdam, Special Lecture Series of the Center of Metropolitan Studies.)

1992   "Four Asian Tigers with a Dragon Head: State Intervention and Economic Development in the Asian Pacific Rim," In Richard Appelbaum and Jeff Henderson (eds), *State and Society in the Pacific Rim*, London: Sage.

"Rusia, Año I: el Presidente en su laberinto." *Política Exterior* (Spring).

1991   "Las tecnologías de la información (1985–1990): España en el contexto mundial" (with M. Gamella). In Roberto Dorado et alt. (eds), *Ciencia, tecnología e industria en España*, Madrid: Fundesco.

"La nueva revolución rusa." *Claves* (October).
"Estrategias de desarrollo metropolitano: la articulación entre crecimiento económico y calidad de vida." In Jordi Borja et al. (eds), *Las grandes ciudades en la década de los noventa*, Madrid: Sistema.
"Die zweigeteilte Stadt – Arm und Reich in den Stadten Lateinamerikanisch, der USA und Europas." In Tilo Schabert (ed.), *Die Welt der Stadt*, Munich and Zurich: Piper, 199–216.
"Informatisierte Stadt und Soziale Bewegungen." In Martin Wentz (ed.), *Stadt-Raume*, Frankfurt: Campus Verlag, 137–48.
"Sotsiologicheskie ocherki." In *Yezhegodnik*, Moscow: Vyshie Sotsiologicheskie Kursi, 7–27.
"Sotsiologiya modernizatsii i ekonomicheskogo razvitia." In *Kurs Lektsii*, Moscow: Vyshie Sotsiologicheskie Kursi, 3–8.
"Modernizatsiya: ekonomika i sotsialnie strukturi." In *Materiali Kruglogo Stola*, Moscow: Vyshie Sotsiologicheskie Kursi.

1990 "El fin del comunismo." *Claves*, 1.
"Vysokie tekhnologii i obschestvo." In *Lektsiya: Vlianie novoi tekhnologii na rabotu i zdanyatost*, Moscow: Vyshie Sotsiologicheskie Kursi.

1989 "The New Dependency: Technological Change and Socio-Economic Restructuring in Latin America" (with Roberto Laserna). *Sociological Forum*, (Fall) (Translated into Spanish, 1990; reprinted in A. D. Kincaid and A. Portes (eds), *Comparative National Development*, Chapel Hill: University of North Carolina press, 1994.
"Nuevas tecnologías y desarrollo regional." *Economía y Sociedad*, 2: 23–40.
"World Underneath: The Origins, Dynamics and Effects of the Informal Economy" (with A. Portes). In A. Portes, M. Castells, and L. Benton (eds), *The Informal Economy*, Baltimore: Johns Hopkins University Press. (Translated into Spanish.)
"Social Movements and the Informational City." *Hitotsubashi Journal of Social Studies*, 21: 197–206. (Translated into Japanese (1989) and German (1991).)
"High Technology and the New International Division of Labour." *Labour Studies* (October).

"High Technology and the Changing International Division of Production: Implications for the U.S. Economy" (with Laura Tyson). In Randall B. Purcell (ed.), *The Newly Industrializing Countries in the World Economy: Challenges for U.S. Policy*, Boulder, Co: Lynne Rienner, 13–50.

1988   "Innovation technologique et centralité urbaine." *Cahiers de la Recherche Sociologique*, 6, 2: 27–36.

"The New Industrial Space. Information Technology Manufacturing and Spatial Structure in the United States." In George Sternlieb and James W. Hughes (eds), *America's Market Geography*, New Brunswich, NJ: Center for Urban Policy Research, Rutgers University.

Nuevas tecnologías, economía y sociedad. Lección inaugural del curso académico 1988–89. Madrid: Universidad Autónoma de Madrid.

Crisis urbana, Estado y participación popular. Lectures. Cochabamba, Bolivia: Colegio de Arquitectos de Cochabamba. 264 pages.

"High Technology Choices Ahead: Restructuring Interdependence" (with Laura Tyson). In John W. Sewell and Stuart K. Tucker (eds), *Growth, Exports and Jobs in a Changing World*, Washington DC: Overseas Development Council, Transaction Books, 55–95.

1987   "Competitività internazionale, innovazione tecnologica e trasferimento di tecnologia in un'economia aperta: l'esperienza della Spagna degli anni ottanta" (with Javier Nadal). In Patrizio Bianchi (ed.), *Crescita e Competitività: Strategie Nazionali*, Bologna: Nomisma, Laboratorio di Politica Industriale.

"Revolución tecnológica y reestructuración económico-política del sistema mundial." In Manuel Castells et al., *Impacto de las tecnologías avanzadas sobre el concepto de seguridad*, Madrid: Fundación de Estudios sobre la Paz y las Relaciones Internacionales.

"Ocho modelos de desarrollo tecnológico." *Nuevo Siglo*, 1: 5–13.

1986   "High Technology and Urban Dynamics in the United States." In Mattei Dogan and John D. Kasarda (eds), *The Metropolis Era*, vol. 1, Beverly Hills, CA: Sage.

"High Technology, World Development and Structural Transformation." *Alternatives*, 11, 3. (Translated into German.)

"Technological Change, Economic Restructuring and the Spatial Division of Labor." In Walter Stohr (ed.), *International Economic Restructuring and the Territorial Community*, Vienna: United Nations Industrial Development Organization.

"The New Urban Crisis." In Dieter Friek (ed.), *The Quality of Urban Life*, Berlin and New York: Walter de Gruyter.

1985   "Urbanization and Social Change: The New Frontier." In Orlando Fals Borda (ed.), *The Challenge of Social Change*, London: Sage Studies in International Sociology, 93–106.

"El impacto de las nuevas tecnologías sobre los cambios urbanos y regionales." In Peter Hall et al., *Metropolis, Territorio y Crisis*, Madrid: H. Blume, 37–62.

"Estado, cultura y sociedad: las nuevas tendencias históricas." In collective author, *Cultura y Sociedad*, Madrid: Ministerio de Cultura.

1984   "Class and Power in American Cities." (Review essay.) *Contemporary Sociology*, 13, 3: 270–3.

"Madrid: planeamiento urbano y gestión municipal." *Ciudad y Territorio* (January–June): 13–40.

"Participation, Politics, and Spatial Innovation: Commentary on Bologna, Orcasitas, and SAAL." In Richard Hatch (ed.), *The Scope of Social Architecture*, vol. 1: Columns, New Jersey Institute of Technology and Van Nostrand.

"After the Crisis?" (with Martin Carnoy). *World Policy Journal* (Spring): 495–516.

1983   "Crisis, Planning, and the Quality of Life." In *Environment and Planning D*, 1, 1: 3–21. (Translated into Portuguese and Spanish.)

1982   "Squatters and Politics in Latin America." In Helen J. Safa (ed.), Towards a Political Economy of Urbanization in Third World Countries, New Delhi: Oxford University Press, 242–62. (Reprinted in Josef Gugler (ed.), *The Urbanization of the Third World*, Oxford: Oxford University Press, 1988.)

"Cultural Identity and Urban Structure: The Spatial Organization of San Francisco's Gay Community" (with Karen Murphy). In *Urban Affairs Annual Reviews*, vol. 22, Beverly Hills, CA: Sage, 237–60.

1981   "Local Government, Urban Crisis, and Political Change." In *Political Power and Social Theory*. A Research Annual, vol. 2, Greenwich, CT, 1–20.

1979   "Revisar a Engels." *Argumentos* (July).
        "La intervención administrativa en los centros urbanos de
        las grandes ciudades." *Revista de Sociología*, 11: 227–50.
1978   "Urban Social Movements and the Struggle for Democracy:
        The Citizen Movement in Madrid." *International Journal of
        Urban and Regional Research*, 2, 1: 133–46.
        "Mouvements sociaux urbains et changement politique." In
        Alain Touraine (ed.), *Mouvements sociaux d'aujourd'hui*,
        Paris: Les Editions Ouvrières.
1977   "Towards a Political Urban Sociology." In Michael Harloe
        (ed.), *Captive Cities*, London: John Wiley, 61–78.
        "Marginalité urbaine et mouvements sociaux au Mexique:
        le mouvement des posesionarios dans la ville de Monter-
        rey." *International Journal of Urban and Regional Research*,
        1, 2: 145–50.
        "Les conditions sociales d'émergence des mouvements
        sociaux urbains." *International Journal of Urban and Regional
        Research*, 1, 1.
        "Apuntes para un análisis de clase de la política urbana del
        Estado mexicano." *Revista Mexicana de Sociología*, 4.
1976   "Crise de l'Etat, consommation collective et contradictions
        urbaines." In Nicos Poulantzas (ed.), *La Crise de l'Etat*, Paris:
        Presses Universitaire de France, 179–208. (Translated into
        Spanish and Danish.)
        "The Wild City." *Kapital-State*, 4–5 (Summer): 1–30.
        (Reprinted in Joe R. Feagin (ed.), *The Urban Scene*, New
        York: Random House, 1979.)
        "Theoretical proposition for an Experimental Study of
        Urban Social Movements." In G. C. Pickvance (ed.),
        Urban Sociology: Critical Essays, London: Tavistock, 147–
        73.
        "The Service Economy and the Post-Industrial Society. A
        Sociological Critique." *International Journal of Health
        Services*, 6, 4: 596–607.
        "La crise urbaine aux Etats-Unis: vers la barbarie?." *Les
        temps modernes* (February): 1178–1240. (Translated into
        Dutch, in book form, Amsterdam: EU, 1978.)
1975   "Advanced Capitalism, Collective Consumption and Urban
        Contradictions." In Leo Lindberg et al. (ed), *Stress and
        Contradiction in Modern Capitalism*, Lexington, MA: Heath,
        175–98.

"Urban Sociology and Urban Politics: From a Critique to New Trends of Research." *Comparative Urban Research*, 3, 1. (Reprinted in John Walton (ed.), *The City in Comparative Perspective*, Beverly Hills, CA: Sage, 1976.)
"La fonction sociale de la planification urbaine: le cas de la région de Dunkerque." *Recherches Sociologiques*, 3.
"Immigrant Workers and Class Struggle: The Western European Experience." *Politics and Society*, 1. (Translated into French.)

1974 "Contradizione e desiguaglianza nella città," *Il Mulino*, 1.
"Consommation collective, interêts de classe et processus politique dans le capitalisme avancé." *Revista de Sociología*, special issue, 63–90.
"Remarques sur le pouvoir local." *Review essay. Revue Française de Sociologie*, June.

1973 "Epistemología y ciencias sociales." *Revista Latinoamericana de Ciencias Sociales*, 1.
"Il rinovo urbano di Parigi: aspetti economici e politici." *Archivio di Studi Urbani e Regionali*, 2.
"Movimiento de pobladores y lucha de clases en Chile." *Revista Latinoamericana de Estudios Urbanos*, 3.
"Tesi sulla questione urbana." *Archivio di Studi Urbani e Regionali*, 1.
"La teoría marxista de las clases sociales y la lucha de clases en América Latina." In collective author, *Las clases sociales en América Latina*, Mexico: Siglo XXI.

1972 "Luttes de classes et contradictions urbaines." *Espaces et Sociétés*, 6–7 (October).
"Symbolique urbaine et mouvements sociaux." *Versus. Studi Semiotici.*

1971 "La sociologie et la question urbaine." *L'architecture d'aujourd'hui* (September): 91–100.
"El mito de la cultura urbana." *Revista Latinoamericana de Estudios Urbanos*, 3: 27–42.
"La détermination des pratiques sociales en situation de retraite." (with Anne-Marie Guillemard). *Sociologie du Travail*, 3.
"L'urbanisation dépendante en Amérique Latine." *Espaces et Sociétés*, 3: 5–23. (Translated into Spanish and Italian.)

1970 "Structures sociales et processus d'urbanisation." *Annales* (August): 1155–99.

"Reconquête urbaine et rénovation-déportation à Paris."
(co-author). *Sociologie du Travail*, 4: 488–514.
"La rénovation urbaine aux Etats-Unis." *Espaces et Sociétés*,
1: 107–37.
"Les nouvelles frontières de la méthodologie sociologique."
Information sur les sciences sociales, 79–108. (Translated into
Portuguese (1973) and Spanish (1972).)
1969 "Le centre urbain." *Cahiers internationaux de sociologie*
(May): 83–106.
"Entreprise industrielle et développement urbain." *Synopsis*
(September): 69–79.
"Vers une théorie sociologique de la planification urbaine."
Sociologie du Travail, 4: 130–43. (Translated into English
(1981) and Spanish (1974).)
"Théorie et idéologie en sociologie urbaine." *Sociologie et
Sociétés*, 2: 171–91. (Translated into English (1976).)
1968 "Y a-t-il une sociologie urbaine?." *Sociologie du Travail*, 1:
72–90. (Translated into English (1976).)
"La mobilité des entreprises industrielles dans la région
parisienne" (co-author). *Cahiers de l'Institut d'Aménagement
et d'Urbanisme de la Région Parisienne*, 11.
1967 "Mobilité des entreprises et structure urbaine." (co-author).
Sociologie du Travail, 4: 369–405.

III. Main Research Monographs, 1984–2002

2002 *La era de la información en América Latina: ¿es sostenible la
globalización?* Ponencia al Seminario sobre la Era de la Información en América Latina, Programa de Naciones Unidas
para el Desarrollo, Santa Cruz, Bolivia, March.
2001 *Diffusion and Uses of Internet in Catalonia and in Spain: A
Commented Summary of available evidence*. Barcelona, Universitat Oberta de Catalunya, Internet Interdisciplinary
Institute, Working Paper, December.
The Finnish Model of Information Society (with Pekka
Himanen). Helsinki: SITRA.
1999 *Russia in the Information Age* (with Emma Kiselyova).
Berkeley: University of California, Center for Slavic Studies,
and Carnegie Foundation.

Globalización, identidad y Estado en América Latina. Santiago de Chile: Programa de Naciones Unidas para el Desarrollo.

1998 *Russia as a Network Society* (with Emma Kiselyova). Stanford, CA: Stanford University Conference on Russia, Conference Proceedings.

1996 *The Missing Link: Siberian Oil & Gas and the Pacific Economy* (with Emma Kiselyova and Alexander Granberg). Berkeley: University of California, Institute of Urban and Regional Development.

1994 a. *La reindustrialización de Asturias; problemas, perspectivas y estrategias,* Oviedo: Presidencia del Principado de Asturias. (Director)
b. *La modernización tecnológica de las empresas industriales de electrónica y telecomunicaciones en Rusia.* Madrid: Universidad Autónoma, Instituto de Sociología de Nuevas Tecnologías, Programa de Estudios Rusos. (Director)
c. *El proceso de cambio político y social en la Rusia post-comunista.* Madrid: Universidad Autonóma, Instituto de Sociología de Nuevas Tecnologías, Programa de Estudios Rusos. (Director)

1993 *Paths Toward the Informational Society: The Transformation of Employment Structure in the G-7 Countries, 1920–2005* (with Yoko Aoyama). Berkeley: University of California, Berkeley Roundtable on the International Economy.

1992 a. *Informe sobre la formación del medio de innovación tecnológica "Cartuja 93"* (Sevilla, Spain) (with Clara García and Isabel Ramos). Seville: Sociedad Estatal Expo '92.
b. Informe-Dictamen sobre el desarrollo sostenible del entorno del Parque Nacional de Donana (Andalusia, Spain). Seville: Junta de Andalucía. (Coordinator)

1991 *The University as Engine of Development in the New World Economy.* Report prepared for the World Bank. Washington, DC: World Bank.

1989 a. *El impacto de las nuevas tecnologías en la economía mundial. Implicaciones para la economía española.* Informe para el Ministerio de Economia, Madrid.
b. *The State and Technological Policy. A Comparative Analysis of the U.S. Strategic Defense Initiative, Informatics Policy in Brazil, and Electronic Policy in China.* Berkeley: University of California, Berkeley Roundtable on the International Economy. (Director)

1988   a. *Economic Modernization and Technology Transfer in the People's Republic of China* (with Martin Carnoy and Patrizio Bianchi). Stanford, CA: Stanford University, School of Education, CERAS.
b. *Desarrollo tecnológico, cooperación internacional y espacios de innovación.* Report prepared for Sociedad Estatal Expo '92. Seville, Spain.

1988   a. *The Developmental City State in an Open World Economy: The Singapore Experience.* Berkeley: University of California, Berkeley Roundtable on the International Economy.
b. *Economic Development and Public Housing in the Asian Pacific Rim: A Comparative Analysis of Hong Kong, Singapore, and Shenzhen Special Economic Zone* (with Reg W. Kwok and Lee Goh). Berkeley: University of California, Institute of Urban and Regional Development.

1987   *The Real Crisis of Silicon Valley.* Santa Cruz: University of California, Silicon Valley Research Group.

1986   a. *Public Housing and Economic Development in Hong Kong.* Hong Kong: University of Hong Kong, Centre of Urban Studies and Planning.
b. *High Technology, Economic Policies, and World Development.* Report prepared for the Committee for a Just World Peace, published by Berkeley Roundtable on the International Economy, University of California.

1985   *El impacto de las nuevas tecnologías sobre la economía y la sociedad en España.* Madrid: Informe para la Presidencia del Gobierno. (Director)

1984   *Towards the Informational City? High Technology, Economic Change, and Spatial Structure.* Berkeley: University of California, Institute of Urban and regional Development.

Biographies of the Authors

Manuel Castells

Born in Spain, 1942, resident in the United States since 1979.

Married to Emma Kiselyova; one daughter, one stepdaughter, three grandchildren.

Professor of City and Regional Planning, and Professor of Sociology, University of California at Berkeley, appointed professor in 1979. At Berkeley he holds or has held these positions:

Chair, Center for Western European Studies (1994–8); member of the Executive Committee, Institute of International Studies (current); member of the Board, Institute for Slavic and Eastern European Studies (former); Berkeley Campus Voting Delegate to NASULGC Commission (former); member of the Executive Committee, College of Environmental Design (former); elected member of the Assembly of the Academic Senate (former); and research fellow of the Institute of Urban and Regional Development, the Institute of European Studies, the Center for Latin American Studies, and the Center for Southeast Asian Studies.

Since 2001 he has been Research Professor at the Universitat Oberta de Catalunya (UOC) in Barcelona.

Academic Career

Researcher, Laboratory of Industrial Sociology, Ecole Pratique des Hautes Etudes, Paris, 1965–7.

Assistant Professor of Sociology, University of Paris (Nanterre Campus), 1967–9.

Assistant Professor of Sociology, University of Montreal, 1969–70.

Assistant Professor of Sociology (with tenure), and director of the Seminar for Urban Sociology, Ecole des Hautes Etudes en Sciences Sociales, Paris, 1970–9.

Professor of Sociology and director, Institute for Sociology of New Technologies, Universidad Autónoma de Madrid, 1988–93.

Research Professor, Consejo Superior de Investigaciones Científicas, Barcelona, 1997.

Research Professor, Internet Interdisciplinary Institute, Universitat Oberta de Catalunya (UOC), Barcelona, 2001– .

Education and University Degrees

Secondary Education in Barcelona, Spain, 1951–8. Studies in Law and Economics, University of Barcelona, 1958–62, interrupted by political exile at the age of 20.

Licence (Master's) in Public Law and Political Economy, Faculty of Law and Economics, University of Paris, 1964.

Diploma in Sociology of Work, Institute of Social Sciences of Work, University of Paris, 1965.

Diplome d'Etudes Approfondies (Master's) in Sociology, Ecole Pratique des Hautes Etudes, University of Paris, 1966.

Doctorat de 3ème cycle (Ph.D.) in Sociology, University of Paris, 1967; Doctorado (Ph.D.) in Sociology, Universidad Complutense de Madrid, 1978; Doctorat d'Etat des Lettres et Sciences Humaines, University of Paris "René Descartes-Sorbonne, 1983." These three doctorates are independent degrees, with different dissertations.

Main Awards, Honors, and Academic Appointments

John H. Simon Guggenheim Fellow, 1982–3.

C. Wright Mills Award from the Society for the Study of Social Problems, for the book *The City and the Grassroots* (University of California Press, 1983).

Robert and Helen Lynd Award for Life Long Contribution to the Field of Urban and Community Sociology, awarded by the American Sociological Association, 1998.

Kevin Lynch Award in Urban Design and Urban Planning from the Massachusetts Institute of Technology, 2001.

Award Fernández de los Ríos for the best essay on urbanism from the Regional Government of Madrid for the book *Technopoles of the World* (Routledge, 1995).

Award for the best book on the Information Society from the Catalan Institute of Technology, Barcelona, 1998.

Madrid Silver Medal of City Planning, from the Regional Government of Madrid, 1999.

Prize for Social Theory, from the Fundació Rafael Campalans (Catalan Trade Unions), Barcelona, 1999.

Internet Cambrescat Award from the Chambers of Commerce of Catalonia for contribution to the understanding of Internet in business and in society, Barcelona, 2000.

Order of the Lion of Finland, from the President of Finland, 2002.

L'ordre des Arts et des Lettres, from the Government of France, 2002.

Doctor Honoris Causa, Universidad Mayor de San Andrés, La Paz, Bolivia, 1998.

Medal of Honor, Universidade de São Paulo, Brazil, 1999.

Doctor Honoris Causa, Universidad de Valencia, Spain, 2001.

Doctor Honoris Causa, Universidad de Castilla-La Mancha, Spain, 2001.

Doctor Honoris Causa, Twente University, The Netherlands, 2001.

Doctor Honoris Causa, Queen's University, Canada, 2002.

Honorary Doctorate, Helsinki University of Technology, 2002.

Appointed Member of the Academia Europaea in 1994.

Main Professional Appointments Outside Academia

Adviser to the US Agency for International Development, the World Bank, the OECD, and the European Union.

Former member of the Spanish Government's Advisory Council on Science and Technology, and adviser of the research program on new technologies for the Prime Minister of Spain, 1984–6.

Chair of the International Advisory Committee on the Social and Political Problems of the Transition for the Prime Minister of Russia, during the first Yeltsin administration, January–December 1992.

Member of the International Advisory Board on Information Technology and Development, to the President of South Africa, 2000– .

Adviser to the governments of Chile (Allende administration), Mexico, Nicaragua, Ecuador, Spain, China, Brazil, Portugal, and Finland.

Member of the Advisory Board, International Institute of Labour Studies, International Labour Office, UN, Geneva, 1993–6.

Member of the European Commission High Level Expert Group on the Information Society, 1995–7.

Member of the Advisory Board of the United Nations Human Development Report, 1998–2001. Member of the Advisory Board to the United Nations Secretary General on Information and Communication Technology, 2000–1. Member of the Advisory Board to the United Nations Secretary General's Task Force on Information and Communication Technology, 2001– .

Visiting Professorships

Castells has held visiting professorships and extended lectureships in the following universities: Flasco-Chile (1968, 1970), Universidad Católica de Chile (1971, 1972), Universidade de Campinas, Brazil (1971), Université de Montreal (1969), Université de Génève (1974), University of California at Santa Guz (1975), University of Wisconsin (1975, 1977), Royal School of Fine Arts in

Copenhagen (1976), Boston University (1976), Universidad Metropolitana de México (1976), Universidad Central de Venezuela (1981), Universidade de Brasilia (1982), Universidad Autónoma Nacional de México (1982), University of Hong Kong (1983, 1987), National University of Singapore (1987), University of Southern California, Los Angeles (1984, 1985, 1986), National University of Taiwan (1989), Center for Advanced Sociology, Moscow (1990, 1991), University of Amsterdam (1992), Hitotsubashi University, Tokyo (1995), Oxford University (2000), Center for Higher Education Transformation, South Africa (2000).

He has given invited lectures in more than 300 universities and academic institutions in 43 countries, including MIT, Harvard, Columbia, Princeton, Pennsylvania, Cornell, Johns Hopkins, Chicago, Stanford, UCLA, USC, London School of Economics, Oxford, Cambridge, Berlin, Frankfurt, Stockholm Technology Institute, Amsterdam, Louvain, Bocconi (Milan), Barcelona, Moscow, Novosibirsk, Beijing, Tokyo, Seoul, Witwatersraand (Johannesburg), UNAM-Mexico, Buenos Aires, Federal de Rio de Janeiro, and São Paulo. Between 1994 and 2001 he gave 75 keynote speeches and distinguished lectures in 19 countries, and in various international academic meetings.

Academic Service (Main Activities)

Member of the Executive Committee of the International Sociological Association, 1990–4.

President of the Research Committee on Sociology of Urban and Regional Development, of the International Sociological Association, 1978–82.

Member of the Editorial Board of 14 academic journals.

Main Research Fields

Sociology and economics of information technology; interdisciplinary analysis of the information society; technology policy; urban sociology; comparative urbanization; regional development; comparative political economy; sociology of social movements.

Main Teaching Fields (Chronological Sequence)

Methodology of social research; urban sociology; sociology of development; sociology of social movements; political economy; social planning; comparative urban policy; regional development; sociology of information technology.

Martin Ince

Martin Ince is a British journalist born in Birkenhead, Merseyside, and living in London. He is contributing editor of the *Times Higher Education Supplement*, where he was previously deputy editor, and a frequent conference and broadcast speaker and media trainer. He has written for many newspapers and magazines. He read geology and chemistry at the University of Newcastle upon Tyne (England) and is a fellow of the Royal Astronomical Society and a member of the Executive Committee of the Association of British Science Writers. He is a visiting fellow at the Sustainable Cities Research Institute, Northumbria University (England).

His previous books are:
Space (Sphere, 1982)
Energy Policy: Britain's Electricity Industry (Junction Books, 1983)
Sizewell Report (Pluto, 1984)
Sizewell B: Under Pressure (FOE Trust, 1986)
Space Wars (a cartoon book illustrated by David Hine, Camden Press, 1986)
The Politics of British Science (Harvester Wheatsheaf, 1986)
The Rising Seas (Earthscan, 1990)
Dictionary of Astronomy (Peter Collin Publishing, 1997; US edition Fitzroy Dearborn, Chicago, 1997; second edition Peter Collin, 2001; online on xrefer+, the foremost online reference service)

Index